If They Give You Lined Paper
If They Give You Lined Paper
If They Give You Lined Paper
If They Give You Lined Paper
If They Give You Lined Paper
If They Give You Lined Paper
If They Give You Lined Paper
If They Give You Lined Paper
If They Give You Lined Paper
If They Give You Lined Paper
If They Give You Lined Paper

Write Sideways

Also by Daniel Quinn

Ishmael

Providence
The Story of a Fifty-Year Vision Quest

The Story of B

My Ishmael

Beyond Civilization
Humanity's Next Great Adventure

After Dachau

The Man Who Grew Young

The Holy

Tales of Adam

Work, Work, Work

If They Give You Lined Paper

Write Sideways

DANIEL
QUINN

STEERFORTH PRESS
Hanover, New Hampshire

For information about permission to reproduce
selections from this book, write to:
Steerforth Press L.C., 25 Lebanon Street,
Hanover, New Hampshire 03755

LIBRARY OF CONGRESS CATALOGING-IN-PUBLICATION DATA
Quinn, Daniel.
  If they give you lined paper, write sideways / Daniel Quinn. — 1st ed.
    p. cm.
  ISBN-13: 978-1-58642-126-7 (alk. paper)
  ISBN-10: 1-58642-126-3 (alk. paper)
  1. Ethnopsychology. 2. Cognition and culture. I. Title.

GN502.Q85 2007
153—dc22

                                                        2006033169

FIRST EDITION

"*There is always a brave new world,*" said Poirot, "*but only, you know, for very special people. The lucky ones. The ones who carry the making of that world within themselves.*"

— AGATHA CHRISTIE

Preface

I N OCTOBER 2005 I received a letter from a reader who was going to be in Houston — my home — over the Thanksgiving weekend; she wondered if she might spend some time with me to nail down the ideas she had explored in my books. I agreed, with the understanding that I had a purpose of my own: I wanted to use our conversation, taped and edited, as the basis for a new book I had in mind.

At her request I have replaced her name with another, of her choosing. What follows is a lightly edited transcript of our dialogue.

Although references are made herein to the fact that I've written other books, the reading of these other books is not in any way a prerequisite to reading this one. To put the matter a different way, in writing this book, I have not assumed that the reader will be familiar with any of the ideas put forward in earlier works.

Thursday: Morning

Elaine [after an exchange of the usual civilities]. As you can imagine, I'm very curious to know about the book you're working on.

Daniel. It would be nearer the truth to describe it as a book I've been struggling with on and off for the past five years — at least. I'll try to explain... When I finished *Ishmael*, I imagined that I'd done what I set out to do a dozen years before. I thought that this was *it* and that my work was done. A very naive notion.

Elaine. Why naive?

Daniel. Because no one with anything important to say has ever managed to encompass the whole of it in one book. What I learned from writing *Ishmael* was how far short I'd fallen. This is what the thousands of letters I received told me. Readers loved the book but came away from it with serious misunderstandings of what I was saying. I thought I could correct those misunderstandings with a second book, *The Story of B*. From the reaction to that book, I saw that a third was needed. That was *My Ishmael: A Sequel*. What I then saw was that a fourth was needed in order to knit all my ideas together in a very simple, straightforward way, and this was *Beyond Civilization*.

Elaine. Uh-huh.

Daniel. When *Beyond Civilization* was still in manuscript form, I agreed to meet with a small group of readers who, like you, asked for an opportunity to get together with me to nail down their understanding of what I was saying. I agreed to give them a long weekend, but they had to arrive having read *Beyond Civilization.* When they arrived, however, it was soon clear that *Beyond Civilization* had answered very nearly all the questions they'd wanted to ask me. The "seminar" was over after about two hours, and we had to spend the rest of the weekend just socializing . . . The point I'm making here is that, with this book, I largely answered the multitude of questions that readers had been asking me ever since *Ishmael* appeared.

Elaine. Yes, I can see that. Though I think your essay "The New Renaissance" was what really did it for me.*

Daniel. Yes. For anyone seeking a concise expression of my basic message, "The New Renaissance" was it. I felt I'd said everything I had to say. But one question remained. This was a question that had been there from the beginning, but for many years I tended to dismiss it.

Elaine. What question was that?

Daniel. "How do you do what you do?"

Elaine. You say you tended to dismiss it . . . ?

Daniel. I dismissed it because I thought the answer was obvious: Anyone who'd worked at it as hard and as long as I had could have done the same.

Elaine. But you changed your mind.

---

*See Appendix I.

Daniel. Yes, reluctantly. Reluctantly because I'd never wanted to put myself forward as someone special or extraordinary.

Elaine. What changed your mind?

Daniel. Experience. I'll give you an example. In the summer of 1998 I tried an experiment. So many people had asked for an opportunity to study with me that I decided to run a nightly summerlong seminar that anyone willing to travel to Houston could attend for as long as they wanted. The attendance naturally fluctuated. During one week, when one group departed and another was expected, a single member of the seminar was stranded by himself, two thousand miles from home, and I felt obliged to look after him. We spent a lot of time just getting to know each other.

At the same time, I felt he should be getting something useful from the experience. He had read all my books many times, with great care and dedication, but still wanted to know if he really had got what I was saying to the extent that he thought he had. To find out, I culled about a hundred of the more interesting questions that had collected on my Web site over the years and let him try to answer them, one by one. We were both astonished by the results of this test. To the vast majority of questions he had no answer at all. He did attempt a few answers, but when these were compared with my own, it was obvious that he and I were not at all on the same page. In other words, what the experiment proved was that, while he knew the answers to questions raised in my books, he couldn't generate *new* answers — answers that were nowhere to be found in my books.

Elaine. Why was this, do you think?

Daniel. We'll come to that ... Meanwhile, here's another example. A few years ago a certain nonprofit group, impressed with my work, invited me to sit in on a planning meeting for an enterprise they were undertaking. I sat and listened as the planning team brainstormed their ideas for several hours. Finally, exhausted, one of them turned to me and said, "Well, Daniel, you've been awfully quiet. What's your take on all this?"

I explained that I wasn't entirely sure of my reaction yet and wanted to let my thoughts settle a bit before speaking.

"Just your gut reaction," they insisted.

Knowing I needed time to formulate my reaction in measured and diplomatic terms, I asked them not to pressure me to speak at that point, but they eventually overrode all my excuses, assuring me that any contribution from me would be welcome.

I told them what I thought, and they stared at me in something very like horror.

Instead of informing them they should have given me the time I asked for (which I needed in order to find a way of expressing myself that would *not* horrify them), I feebly justified myself by saying that if I had any reason to be at such a meeting, it was to view the proceedings as a complete outsider would — as a Martian anthropologist would, in fact. With as much cordiality as they could muster, they agreed this was exactly what they wanted me to do.

There are, of course, no such things as Martians, as the folks at this meeting knew perfectly well, but they understood what I meant all the same. In fact, I later learned from an insider that members of this group are now encouraged to "think like Martians." But the original Martian anthropologist has never been invited to another meeting.

Elaine. What's your theory? Why were they horrified by what you had to say?

Daniel. One more example will answer this question. A few months ago I had a telephone conference with a group of readers in Tulsa. One of the participants made an observation that seems quite commonplace but that had a telling effect on me. He said, approximately, "What are we supposed to do? When we talk to people, we're each speaking from some conventional frame of reference. What we don't understand or share is *your* frame of reference. Your frame of reference seems completely alien and mysterious to us."

Suddenly I felt I had a handle on the problem. Obvious as it seems in retrospect, it was my frame of reference that was different. The young man I talked about a minute ago couldn't answer questions the way I did because he didn't share my frame of reference, and the members of the corporate group I just described were horrified because they were looking at the matter under discussion from a frame of reference that was completely different from mine.

Elaine. So what *is* your frame of reference? Or can you describe it?

Daniel. What I have is a shorthand for it. My frame of reference is that of a Martian anthropologist. I'm like someone who has traveled millions of miles to study a species of beings who, while supposedly rational, are destroying the very planet they live on.

Elaine. Wow. Okay. And how do you describe the frame of reference of a Martian anthropologist?

Daniel. I don't really think a description would help you much — even if I knew how to provide one. To learn how to swim, you must swim. It's not something that can be described. Someone has to throw you into the water.

Elaine [smiling]. That sounds exciting.

Daniel. It may help you to hear how I evolved into what I've become. It was certainly not by any sort of choice or desire on my part. I had not the slightest inclination to single myself out in any way.

Elaine. I think I understand.

Daniel. I remember how it began quite exactly. It was in about 1962, at the height of the Cold War, when every year or so newspapers would show, on a map of your city, the devastation that would be wrought by the explosion of a hydrogen bomb. The idea that a nuclear holocaust could occur at any moment, with the US and Soviet Union raining down nuclear warheads on each other, was not in the least far-fetched, and it was a commonplace saying that, if such a thing happened, we would be blasted back to the Stone Age. Does that sound familiar?

Elaine. I'm not sure I know what you mean.

Daniel. Haven't you ever heard of anyone talking about nuking somebody back to the Stone Age?

Elaine. Yeah. I think some general said we should just go ahead and nuke the North Vietnamese back to the Stone Age.

Daniel. And does that make sense to you?

Elaine. Again, I'm not quite sure I know what you mean.

Daniel. If we'd dropped a dozen hydrogen bombs on North Korea, would they be nuked back to the Stone Age?

Elaine. I'd have to think so.

Daniel. Suppose I said that if we dropped a dozen hydrogen bombs on North Korea, they'd be nuked back to the Middle Ages. Would that make sense to you?

Elaine. No.

Daniel. What made sense was the Stone Age. It made sense to everyone but me, because I knew we wouldn't be able function at anything like the Stone Age level. Do you see why?

Elaine [after a long pause]. It would be pointless to say that I do.

Daniel. Stone Age peoples live very well, where they've been left alone. They were living very well throughout the New World when Europeans began to arrive in the fifteenth century. They fed, clothed, and sheltered themselves almost effortlessly. You have to know that.

Elaine. Yes.

Daniel. If I gave you a sharp cutting tool, a strong needle, some strong thread, and a wide sheet of supple leather, could you make yourself a leather skirt?

Elaine. I think so.

Daniel. But suppose you had none of these tools and materials. For example, could you make a cutting tool sharp enough to cut leather?

Elaine. No.

Daniel. Could you make a needle strong enough to pierce the leather?

Elaine. From scratch? No.

Daniel. Could you make some thread strong enough to hold the leather together?

Elaine. Again, from scratch, no. I wouldn't even know where to begin.

Daniel. And of course, most critically, could you produce the leather?

Elaine. No.

Daniel. Stone Age peoples have all the tools they need to support themselves in a comfortable lifestyle — not a lifestyle that you or I might find comfortable but one that *they* found comfortable. They had not only the tools — hundreds of them — but the knowledge of how to *make* the tools. Whereas you and I, along with 99.99 percent of our population, have none of this knowledge. I myself couldn't even make a piece of string from scratch.

Elaine. Right.

Daniel. So what would happen in the event of a nuclear holocaust? Would we be blasted back to the Stone Age?

Elaine. No.

Daniel. We'd be blasted back to an age that has no name at all. *Homo habilis*, our earliest ancestors, had more skills than we would have, because they *evolved* with those skills. Without them, they couldn't have evolved in the first place.

Elaine. Yes, I can see that.

Daniel. This may seem like a rather trivial point, but it's only a starting point — my own personal starting point. Making this observation was the beginning of my career as a Martian anthropologist. The question I asked myself — and it's an anthropologist's question — was "What are these people thinking when they say that we'd be blasted back to the Stone Age in a nuclear holocaust?"

Elaine. What are they *thinking?*

Daniel. What's the mindset *behind* the statement?

Elaine shakes her head.

Daniel. What's their imaginary picture of the Stone Age condition?

Elaine. Okay, I see where you're going. Or I think I do. What they're seeing when they think of the Stone Age is: no electricity, no radios, no televisions, no central heating, no computers, no telephones.

Daniel. An absence. A nothingness. I'm not talking about *informed opinion* here. But even the well informed would be shocked ten years later, when Marshall Sahlins wrote a seminal book calling Stone Age peoples "the first affluent society." But I'm not talking about *ill-informed* opinion, either. Well-educated people — readers of sophisticated magazines like *The New Yorker* — expected to see cartoons depicting our ancestors living in caves, the males armed with clubs, dragging their mates home by the hair. This was the general, cultural impression.

Elaine. I don't think it's changed much.

Daniel. You're probably right. I haven't really been checking.

Elaine. You say this was the general, cultural impression. Why wasn't it yours?

Daniel. It wasn't mine only because I questioned the received wisdom that a nuclear holocaust would throw us back to the Stone Age. I knew that we wouldn't be so lucky. It would throw

us back into an age of total helplessness, where not one in ten
million of us would know even as much as how to make a piece
of string from scratch.

Elaine. But why did that *occur* to you?

Daniel. That I can't say. It doesn't seem to me to represent a
stroke of genius. I doubt that I ever even mentioned it to anyone. If I had, they probably would have wondered why an intelligent person would expend mental effort on such a trivial
matter.

Elaine. True.

Daniel. But you might say that discovering this bit of nonsense
awakened the Martian anthropologist in me. It was just a loose
thread, but pulling on it I began to unravel the fabric of our culture's received wisdom. This impression of nothingness that
attached to the people from whom we ascended wasn't limited
to the matter of nuclear holocaust. It was part of our general
understanding of the human story.

Like everyone else, I'd had world history as a required course,
and I'd retained into adulthood only one striking, world-shaking
event: the Agricultural Revolution. If something had come
before it, it was at best a hazy nothingness. There obviously had
to be people there, but they were of no consequence. What was
of consequence was the Agricultural Revolution. That was It.
That was the single most momentous event in human history. It
was the beginning of everything that happened of human
importance . . . I began to take note of capsule tellings of the
human story, in books, newspapers, and magazines. Some of
these were written by or quoted from actual historians. They
went something like this: "Humans lived as hunter-gatherers for
some three million years, then, about ten thousand years ago

they abandoned hunting-gathering for the agricultural life, laying the groundwork for civilization."

Elaine. Uh-huh.

Daniel. And what does that "uh-huh" mean?

Elaine. It means, let's see . . . It means I recognize that telling of the story.

Daniel. And do you recognize what's wrong with it?

Elaine. It implies that humanity itself, as a whole, abandoned the hunting-gathering life and took up agriculture about ten thousand years ago.

Daniel. Which is obviously false. Ninety-five hundred years after humanity supposedly abandoned the hunting-gathering life, about three-quarters of the earth's landmass was still occupied by hunter-gatherers who had never heard of or participated in the Agricultural Revolution. Eight or ten years ago I read an article in *Scientific American* that in its introductory paragraphs repeated almost verbatim the conventional description of humanity's abandonment of the hunting-gathering life ten thousand years ago. It didn't occur to me at the time that I might at some future date have use for it, so I'm afraid I didn't make a note of the issue. I wrote a letter to the editors, pointing out the evident absurdity of the description, but of course it wasn't printed. The conventional fable was good enough science for them.

Elaine. Martian anthropologists need not apply.

Daniel. I guess not. But where are we at this point? We know that the story of "world history" generally accepted in our culture is false to facts. Even historians who should know better recite it without giving it a second thought. A respected scientific journal sees no reason not to include it as the introduction to an article. Where does a Martian anthropologist go from here? What is his next question?

Elaine [*after giving the question some thought*]. I'd say his next question is . . . No, I have to say I don't know.

Daniel. Think about this. Aside from a relatively small minority of religious fanatics, the story of the universe as told by present-day science is generally accepted by the people of our culture. The universe was born in a "big bang" some thirteen billion years ago, and our own planet was formed about five billion years ago. Is that right?

Elaine. Is what right?

Daniel. That the people of our culture generally accept this story of the universe, which is not a mythological story or a religious story but a scientific one.

Elaine. Yes, I'd say so, except, as you say, by a few religious fanatics.

Daniel. This story, as far as the most brilliant minds of our time can tell us, is not false to facts.

Elaine. That's right.

Daniel. But the people of our culture accept a story of "world history" — world *human* history — that *is* false to facts. What does a Martian anthropologist think of this?

Elaine. That it's odd.

Daniel. And his question is . . . ?

Elaine. Why? How did it come about that . . .

Daniel. Take your time.

Elaine. How did it come about that the same people who accept without question a scientific history of the universe also embrace a false version of human history?

Daniel. The true version of human history is that humanity did not all at once, ten thousand years ago, abandon the hunting-gathering life for the agricultural life. The hunting-gathering life persisted over three-quarters of the globe until some five hundred years ago — and still persists where it hasn't as yet been stamped out. What is there in this true version of events that alarms us?

Elaine thinks about this.

Daniel. What is there in it that disturbs our settled vision of ourselves?

Elaine sighs in frustration.

Daniel. Don't be distressed if the answers to these questions don't pop right out at you. It took me years to work them out . . . Let's come at it from a different angle. When did we begin to put together our version of the human story?

Elaine. I would guess not more than twenty-five hundred years ago.

Daniel. That's when the foundation thinkers of our culture began to appear: Herodotus, Thucydides, Socrates, Aristotle, and so on.

Elaine. Yes, that's what I was thinking.

Daniel. But of course the fundamental outline of the story might have been in place for thousands of years before that. Everyone in the civilized world knew that there was a human past of *some* kind. The cities the Sumerians inhabited in 3000 BC weren't built in the previous generation or the generation before that. And they could see that the cities were growing and developing technologically. From this, they could logically project backward to a time when the cities were just villages and technologies were very primitive. But what they could not possibly imagine was that these villages were born in a revolution, the one we call the Agricultural Revolution. They couldn't possibly imagine that, before people became farming villagers, they had lived for millions of years in an entirely different way. The hunting-gathering lifestyle was five thousand years in the past, totally forgotten by now. Not even a rumor of it could have survived for that long.

Elaine. Yes, I see that. You called this the Great Forgetting in *The Story of B.*

Daniel. So it had to seem to them that the human story must have begun just a few thousand years before, that being the period of time between those first farming villagers and themselves. On this basis, what conclusion would it have been reasonable for them to draw about the nature of humans as a species?

Elaine. I'm afraid I can't begin to guess what you're getting at here.

Daniel. It's safe to assume that these ancients were as knowledgeable about the creatures around them as we are — probably more so. For example, they must have known that birds hunt insects and build nests. What conclusion would it have been reasonable for them to draw about the nature of birds as a species?

Elaine. I'm tempted to say that they would conclude that it's the nature of birds to hunt insects and build nests.

Daniel. Of course. Birds had been doing that for as long as anyone knew. They must also have known that bees gather nectar and build hives. And what would they conclude from that?

Elaine. That bees are nectar gatherers and hive builders.

Daniel. That's what bees had been doing for as long as anyone knew. And what had humans been doing for as long as anyone knew?

Elaine. Planting crops and building cities.

Daniel. And from that what would they reasonably conclude about the nature of humans?

Elaine. That they are agriculturalists and civilization builders.

Daniel. To them, planting crops and building cities had to seem as innate to humans as gathering nectar and building hives is to bees.

Elaine. Yes.

Daniel. The idea that humans had come into being as tribal hunter-gatherers — planting no crops and building no cities for millions of years — would have seemed preposterous to them.

Elaine. I'd have to think so.

Daniel. Of course we can only conjecture that the Sumerians believed that Man was just a few thousand years old and had been born an agriculturalist and a civilization builder. But it's not conjecture that this story was still in place in our culture four thousand years later, and for centuries of years beyond that. It was the prevailing belief right through the eighteenth century that Man was just a few thousand years old and had been an agriculturalist and a civilization builder from birth.

Elaine. Not quite from birth, but the very first human, Adam, *became* an agriculturalist.

Daniel. Granted. But even in this biblical version of the story, there's no suggestion that the first agriculturalist had been preceded by fifteen or twenty thousand generations of hunter-gatherers.

Elaine. Certainly not. We were agriculturalists from the very first generation — according to the biblical story.

Daniel. Now at last we're poised to give our Martian anthropologist the answer to his first, overriding question. Current in our culture is this version of human history: Humanity is some three million years old, but nothing of consequence happened until we abandoned the hunting-gathering life and became agriculturalists and civilization builders. How did we end up with this story, prefaced by three million years in which nothing of consequence happened?

Elaine. You're asking me to reconstruct it?

Daniel. Give it a try.

Elaine. Wow. Okay. During the nineteenth century new scientific discoveries made it untenable to think that life on earth was just a few thousand years old.

Daniel. Archbishop Ussher's famous calculation, announced in 1654, that the human race was born in 4004 BC, became scientifically untenable. Or rather, to be safe, we can say that it became untenable to those who find scientific evidence more convincing than the belief structure on which Archbishop Ussher made his calculation.

Elaine. Yes.

Daniel. The result was that, among those who generally accepted the evidence of geology and paleobiology — and with it the emerging theory of evolution — the human story had to be revised. It was no longer going to be accepted that Man had been born an agriculturalist and civilization builder just a few thousand years ago.

Elaine. No.

Daniel. And so how was it revised?

Elaine. It was revised to the present version: Humans were around for three million years as hunter-gatherers, but they were of no importance until they abandoned the hunting-gathering life for the agricultural life, beginning about ten thousand years ago.

Daniel. Why was it important to sweep the first three million years of the human story under the rug in this way? Important to the people of our culture, of course.

Elaine. I'll have to think about that . . . I guess I have to say that they honestly saw nothing of value in them.

Daniel. Did anyone look?

Elaine. No one that I'm aware of, but that might not prove anything.

Daniel. You're aware of Darwin and his importance to the history of human thought.

Elaine. Of course.

Daniel. It was imperative that *someone* make sense of the startling discoveries of the young science of paleobiology. If it hadn't been Darwin, it would have been Alfred Russel Wallace. The existence of these findings *demanded* a reasonable explanation, and this explanation would rattle a lot of cages. It wasn't going to go unnoticed.

Elaine. True . . . but I'm not quite sure what point you're making.

Daniel. Paleobiology ultimately made it clear that 99 percent of the human story was played out before the Agricultural Revolution, but no one you can name tried to make sense of it.

Elaine. No.

Daniel. Let's make a conjecture: There was no *felt need* for anyone to make sense of it.

Elaine. I'd say that was right.

Daniel. But why? Why were the people of our culture content to sweep the first three million years of the human story under the rug and leave them there?

Elaine. Okay, I see where you're going now.

Daniel. But what's the answer? I said a few minutes ago that we were at last poised to give our Martian anthropologist the answer to his first, overriding question. Now we're there: Why did the people of our culture — the vanguard and beneficiaries of the Agricultural Revolution — sweep the first three million years of the human story under the rug and leave them there?

Elaine [after some thought]. Those three million years of human history threatened us.

Daniel. In what way? Now you've got to start working as an anthropologist. The people of our culture don't want to think about the fact that, for the first three million years of human life, people lived as hunter-gatherers rather than as agriculturalists and civilization builders. What's behind this reluctance?

Elaine. It's a threat to our self-image.

Daniel. Go on.

Elaine. The story we tell ourselves is that being *fully* human means planting crops and building civilization. This makes us the only *true* humans. In order to maintain our status as the only *true* humans, we don't want to look at the humanity of our hunting-gathering ancestors. We want to *deny* their humanity. They weren't in any real sense humans at all. They were just Stone Age brutes. So we don't have to think about them.

Daniel. To accord them humanity is to deny that we — and we alone — are humanity, which is an important element of our cultural mythology.

Elaine. Yes, that's it.

Daniel. To be human is to live the way we live. This is the one *right* way for people to live, and everyone in the world must be made to live the way we live. It was our holy duty to destroy all the aboriginal cultures we found in the New World, in Australia, in Africa, and so on.

Elaine. That's right.

Daniel [*after a pause*]. Obviously we haven't been breaking new ground here, but that wasn't my purpose. I wanted to give you some insight into my development as a Martian anthropologist, into the path I followed to assemble the answers found in

Ishmael and my other books. I began with a rather trivial observation, that a nuclear holocaust would throw us much farther back than the Stone Age, and from there went from point to point to discover that, according to our cultural mythology, there is only one right way for people to live — our way — and that everyone in the world must be made to live this way. Globalization isn't a recent policy; it's been in place among us for thousands of years.

Elaine. Yes, I can see that.

Daniel. I think we should take a break here. I'd like to know what your reaction to this first session has been.

Elaine. Well, I came hoping to nail down some of your ideas — to settle them in my head. And this has had that effect to some extent. Obviously we've just scratched the surface.

Daniel. I'm glad it's had that effect, but my own purpose is to explore my *method,* if that's what it is. This is the question that has remained unanswered ever since *Ishmael* came out: How did I come to have these ideas? For me they're just the product of hard work and inquiry, but to others they come as revelations. You can't imagine the hundreds of letters I've had from people who tell me that I've turned their world upside down.

Elaine. So what exactly are you asking?

Daniel. I'm asking if I've given you any insight into the workings of my mind — into the workings of the mind of a Martian anthropologist.

Elaine [after giving the matter some thought]. I guess I have to say *some* insight, yes. But the way you approach problems —

Daniel [interrupting]. My "frame of reference."

Elaine. Yes. That remains a mystery. I couldn't do it myself.

Daniel. I wouldn't expect you to at this point. We're just beginning the journey. Before we break for lunch, I'd like to set you a challenge.

Elaine. Okay.

Daniel. As I pointed out a while ago, acknowledging that humanity existed for three million years before *we* came along conflicts with our cultural mythology, which insists that we, the beneficiaries and promoters of the Agricultural Revolution, are humanity itself. You understand that, while the Agricultural Revolution began ten thousand years ago, it didn't *end* then. It's still being carried forward today as we continue to clear land for crops to grow food for ourselves.

Elaine. Yes, I understand that.

Daniel. The idea that humans were around for three million years before us threatens our cultural mythology, but it threatens something much more fundamentally important than that. I want you to examine our culture like a Martian anthropologist and see if you can come up with it. To do this, you'll have think about all the essential elements of our culture, all the constituent parts of it.

Elaine [after another long pause]. I'm afraid I'm drawing a blank.

Daniel. To think like a Martian anthropologist, you have to float high above and look at the whole bunch of us — Americans, Chinese, East Indians, Arabs, Europeans — to discover why affirming the humanity of our ancient ancestors poses a deeper and more immediate threat to us than anything we've discussed so far. I could easily lead you to it with hints, but I don't want to do that. However long it takes, I want you to make this discovery on your own.

Elaine [after a pause]. I guess this leaves me feeling rather at sea.

Daniel. You came here in a passive capacity: to take in what I have to teach. But I want you to leave with more than that. I want you to leave with the ability to do what I do. That won't happen if I just give you all the answers — or if I lead you to the answers through a carefully sequenced series of questions the way Ishmael did with Alan [in *Ishmael*] and Julie [in *My Ishmael*].

Elaine. Yes, I can see that. But all the same . . .

Daniel. Yes . . . ?

Elaine. It's daunting.

Thursday: Afternoon

Daniel. Any progress?

Elaine. You mean on the question you posed? No. I have the feeling I don't really understand it.

Daniel. Acknowledging that humanity existed for three million years before we came along conflicts with our cultural mythology, as you pointed out. But it poses a more dangerous threat than this.

Elaine. To whom?

Daniel. If I give you this, then I may as well give you the whole thing. This is probably too challenging a test for you to begin with. Don't let it worry you. You need more experience with easier tasks.

Elaine. Okay.

Daniel. A few years ago a reader wrote to me to express his surprise at what seemed to him all the dumb questions being asked on my Web site. For him, everything I was saying seemed quite simple: Anything we humans do that disturbs the balance of Nature must be eliminated from our way of life.

Elaine. Uh-huh.

Daniel. What does this "uh-huh" mean? Are you agreeing with him?

Elaine [disconcerted]. Well, yes, I guess so. In a general way.

Daniel. In a general way. In other words, stated in a general way, what Daniel Quinn is saying is that anything we humans do that disturbs the balance of Nature must be eliminated from our way of life.

Elaine. I take it you don't agree.

Daniel. Agreement isn't the point. The two of you share a frame of reference, and that's what we have to examine. To put it another way, the Martian anthropologist asks himself, "What's behind this statement? What's in their minds that leads them to say this? What are they thinking?" Or, to put it an even better way, "What does this statement reveal about their vision of the way world works?"

Elaine sighs.

Daniel. You're frustrated.

Elaine. Yes, I guess so. I came here thinking I had a pretty good grasp of your vision of the way the world works.

Daniel. It's not my particular vision. I mean it's not a vision that's peculiar to me. It's a vision generally accepted in the world of science.

Elaine. What's the statement again?

Daniel. Anything we humans do that disturbs the balance of Nature must be eliminated from our way of life.

Elaine. It seems to me to be a statement that a great many people would agree with.

Daniel. You're probably right. That's what we're looking at: the frame of reference that a great many people — possibly even a majority of people — share. That's the anthropologist's task . . . I've been thinking of this as a book title for a good many years: *If They Give You Lined Paper, Write Sideways.*

Elaine laughs.

Daniel. If you were to pass around a sheet of lined paper with this statement on it, most people would probably write on the next line, "Yes, that's right." I turn the paper sideways and write something else on it.

Elaine. What would you write on it?

Daniel [shaking his head]. The lines on the lined paper represent assumptions or, you might say, the received wisdom of our culture. What is the assumption on which this statement is written? — Anything we humans do that disturbs the balance of Nature must be eliminated from our way of life.

Elaine. Disturbing the balance of Nature is . . . harmful.

Daniel. To what?

Elaine. To . . . the stability of the world. To life.

Daniel. In other words, disturbing the balance of Nature disturbs the balance of Nature.

Elaine [laughs]. Yes, I guess so.

Daniel. But in any case, it's bad.

Elaine. Yes.

Daniel. All right. This is the activity of the Martian anthropologist — or perhaps you could say the method of the Martian anthropologist — to pull away, to pull back and look at the whole.

Elaine. Okay.

Daniel. Pull back four hundred million years and look at the life of the world as it was then. Do you have any kind of picture of it?

Elaine. Not an educated one. I'm not even sure . . . Let's just say I'm not sure where things stood.

Daniel. Well, briefly, land plants began to appear about four hundred million years ago, presumably spreading from lowland swamps. These were followed onto the land by arthropods and other invertebrate groups, and land vertebrates evolved from freshwater fish some forty million years later.

Elaine. Okay.

Daniel. Now repeat after me: Anything that disturbs the balance of Nature is bad.

Elaine, perplexed, says nothing.

Daniel. The appearance of plants on the land disturbed the balance of Nature.

Elaine. Yes, I guess so.

Daniel. You *guess* so? Obviously it did. If it hadn't, all life would still be in the sea. True?

Elaine. Yes.

Daniel. Disturbance of the "balance of Nature" is the driving force of evolution. It is what makes evolution occur. If Nature, as it's called, had ever achieved perfect balance, then evolution would have come to a halt. Mammals were an unimportant class living in the shadows during the dinosaur age. The end of that age opened the way for mammalian development, including the evolution of primates. Now, again, repeat after me: Anything that disturbs the balance of Nature is bad.

Elaine. I can't, of course. Now.

Daniel. So what is your answer going to be to this reader's statement? Anything we humans do that disturbs the balance of Nature must be eliminated from our way of life.

Elaine. It makes no sense.

Daniel. It makes no sense because it's based on a false assumption: that Nature is, or was, balanced until we came along to unbalance it. In order to assent to the policy recommended by this reader, we would have to deny reality and start talking nonsense.

Elaine. I think I'm beginning to get it.

Daniel. What?

Elaine. What it means to think like a Martian anthropologist.

Daniel. Good. Let's move on in a different direction . . . I've already mentioned that Marshall Sahlins described Stone Age peoples as the first affluent society. They lived a life of ease, compared with ours. Contrary to the popular misconception, they didn't live on the knife-edge of survival. To put it in technical terms, they expended far fewer calories to stay alive than their agricultural descendants. In fact, the more people are dependent on cultivated food, the harder they have to work. Obviously it's less work to gather fruit that's growing wild than it is to plant, cultivate, and guard an orchard; less work to gather vegetables that are growing wild than it is to plant, cultivate, guard, and harvest crops.

Elaine. Yes, that much I know.

Daniel. In *Ishmael* and elsewhere I pointed out that, in addition to this, tribal peoples have a life they enjoy living. Since the tribe is not a hierarchical organization, they don't have the frustration of dealing with societal organizations that seem to function like opponents — police, courts, governments, tax collectors, and so on. Factually speaking, where their culture hasn't been undermined by our own, they're not constantly struggling with anxiety, rage, depression, drug addiction, and crime. This isn't to say that they're sweeter, more spiritual, more high-minded, more generous, or more selfless than we are. They're just as susceptible to selfishness, temper tantrums, bad judgment, and violence as we are, though they have a different way of handling these things than we do.

Elaine nods.

Daniel. Reading this, a great many readers write to me demanding to know if I'm saying that we should go back to living in caves and hunting our dinners with a spear.

Elaine. Yes?

Daniel. What's your reaction to this?

Elaine. You've never said anything like that. In fact, you've said very explicitly that that's *not* what you're saying.

Daniel. Of course they're also reacting to the point I've made about the consequences of the Agricultural Revolution. Any population of any species grows and declines as its food resources grow and decline. The Agricultural Revolution allowed us to make sure that our food resources *never* declined. On the contrary, the Agricultural Revolution assured that our food resources could *always* be increased — and in fact have been increased constantly from the beginning of the revolution to the present, so that our population has increased constantly as well. Every increase in population has been met with an increase in food production, which stimulates yet another increase in population.

Elaine. Yes . . . ?

Daniel. And so people write to me to ask, "Are you saying we should go back to living in caves and hunting our dinners with a spear?"

Elaine. Even though you've said specifically that that's not what you're saying.

Daniel. That's right. What am I to make of this? What do *you* make of it?

Elaine. I guess that . . , some people are just not good readers. They just see what they want to see.

Daniel. There's an element of truth in that, to be sure. But I think there's something deeper to be found here.

Elaine [*after a pause*]. I don't know where to look.

Daniel. Pull back. Try to see what's behind the question. Try to see what's going on in the minds of the people who ask it.

Elaine [after a longer pause]. I don't know if I'm on the track here or not, but . . . when the surgeon general reports that smokers are more likely to contract lung cancer than nonsmokers, it's understood that you'd better give up smoking.

Daniel. The description implies a prescription.

Elaine. Yes, that's it.

Daniel. If I point out that tribal peoples generally lead easier, less stressful lives, this is just a description, but some people assume it must be a prescription.

Elaine. That's right.

Daniel. If I point out that the Agricultural Revolution has brought about a boom in human population growth that has brought us to the verge of catastrophe, this is also just a description, but some people assume it must be a prescription — of some kind. For example, some people think I'm saying we should cut food production and let people starve.

Elaine. Well, I have to admit I wondered about that myself.

Daniel. You wondered what my prescription is.

Elaine. Yes.

Daniel. This has been a continuing problem for me — maybe you could call it the anthropologist's dilemma. If I *describe* something, simply doing my job as an anthropologist, it's often assumed that I must also be *prescribing* something.

Elaine. Well, people do *want* prescriptions.

Daniel. That's certainly true . . . I've described the problem as a food race, similar to the arms race between the United States and the Soviet Union during the Cold War . In that arms race, every advance made on our side was answered by an advance on their side, which of course had to be answered by yet another advance on our side, provoking another advance on their side — a never-ending escalation. The food race is the same. Every advance on the side of food production is answered by an advance in population growth, which must be answered by an advance in food production, provoking yet another advance in population growth. For this I *did* have a prescription. The Cold War arms race ended when the Soviet Union simply walked away from it — refused to go on racing with us. The food race could end in the same way, if we simply walked away from it, refused to perpetuate the race between food production and population growth.

Elaine. What would be the result of that?

Daniel. If x amount of food feeds six billion of us this year, then x amount of food will feed six billion of us next year. Won't it?

Elaine. I would think so.

Daniel. And if x amount of food will feed six billion of us next year, then x amount of food will feed six billion of us the year after that, won't it?

Elaine. Yes.

Daniel. Then why increase food production?

Elaine [after a bit of thought]. Ah! To feed the starving millions!

Daniel. Of course. So last year they increased food production in order to feed the starving millions.

Elaine. I assume they did.

Daniel. You can bet on it. So this year the starving millions are being fed, right?

Elaine. No.

Daniel. How long the starving millions have been around I don't know, but from my own personal experience, I can tell you that they've been around for seventy years. And we've been increasing food production for all those years to feed them. But they never get fed, do they?

Elaine. Apparently not.

Daniel. Why not? If we're constantly increasing food production in order to feed them, why are they still starving?

Elaine. That I don't know.

Daniel. I think you do. Or at least I think you know the conventional wisdom about it. That's where the Martian anthropologist has to begin, with the conventional wisdom that everyone accepts without question. The food is there. Everyone agrees that we've got enough food to feed everyone on the planet. But the starving millions go on starving, and the question is, why?

Elaine. The food isn't getting to them.

Daniel. Obviously. But why? Don't the trains and the roads run that far? Aren't there any ports where they live?

Elaine. I don't know.

Daniel. You're stuck in your conventional mental framework, Elaine. You've got to pull back and see it from a distance. Reject the conventional wisdom, with its conventional implications. Think like a Martian anthropologist.

Elaine spends a few minutes at it and then shakes her head.

Daniel. I told you to reject the conventional wisdom, along with its conventional implications. What is the conventional wisdom?

Elaine. That the food is there, it's just not getting to them.

Daniel. The implication being . . .

Elaine. The problem is distribution. The food is not being distributed to the starving.

Daniel. Why? Because of short train lines, blocked roads, closed ports?

Elaine. No.

Daniel. Then why? Is it just some kind of bureaucratic inefficiency?

Elaine. I don't know. Maybe.

Daniel. I'm going to check my e-mail and leave you alone to think about it, okay?

Elaine. Okay.

Daniel [half an hour later]. So. Make any progress?

Elaine. I think so.

Daniel. Go ahead.

Elaine. I pulled back, and what I saw was that the starving millions don't just lack food, they lack everything — food, clothing, shelter.

Daniel. Don't live in oceanside villas and drive BMWs but just happen to be starving.

Elaine. No. They're the poorest of the poor.

Daniel. So the problem isn't that the food isn't reaching them. The problem is that they have no money to buy it. There are no starving rich people.

Elaine. That's right.

Daniel. And how does increasing food production help them?

Elaine. It doesn't. No matter how much food we produce, they're still too poor to buy it.

Daniel. It's well known, of course, that the slowest-growing segment of our population is found in the developed, rich nations.

Elaine. Yes, I've certainly been told that.

Daniel. So where is the growth taking place?

Elaine. Among the poorer, undeveloped nations.

Daniel. Where the starving millions live.

Elaine. That's right.

Daniel. So as we increase food production and our population grows, year after year, where does the greatest part of that growth occur?

Elaine. Among the poorer, undeveloped nations.

Daniel. And in the poorer, undeveloped nations, among what classes do you suppose population growth is slowest?

Elaine. I'd assume it's slowest among the wealthier classes.

Daniel. And where do you suppose it's the fastest?

Elaine. I'd assume it would be the fastest among the poor.

Daniel. Among whom are the starving millions.

Elaine. Yes. But —

Daniel. Yes?

Elaine. It's going to be pointed out that we *do* send them food.

Daniel. And so the starving millions aren't actually starving.

Elaine thinks about this.

Daniel. Are the starving millions starving or not?

Elaine. I guess I have to say that they're starving.

Daniel. If they weren't, why would we be increasing food production every year in order to feed them?

Elaine [after some thought]. It makes no sense.

Daniel. What doesn't?

Elaine. Our rationale for constantly increasing food production.

Daniel. We're not creating a world without hunger?

Elaine. No.

Daniel. Let's be realistic for a moment. Do you honestly believe that the companies spending tens or hundreds of millions a year to develop genetically modified foods are doing so altruistically, motivated by the thought of ending hunger?

Elaine. It would seem unlikely. They're motivated by the thought of making more money.

Daniel. The scientists who do the actual work may imagine that they're working to end world hunger, but I doubt that the top executives have any such notion.

Elaine. I'm sure you're right.

Daniel. And what about the farmers who plant higher-yield crops? Are they doing it to help feed the starving millions?

Elaine. No, realistically, higher yields mean bigger profits, and I have to assume that's what they're thinking about.

Daniel. In 1960 there were three billion of us. Over the next forty years, while we continuously increased food production to feed the starving millions, the starving millions just went on starving. So where was that extra food going?

Elaine. It was going into growing our population.

Daniel. In forty years our population doubled to six billion. So have we demolished the idea that we increase food production every year in order to feed the starving millions?

Elaine. Yes, as far as I'm concerned. What puzzles me is . . .

Daniel. Yes?

Elaine. It seems almost unbelievable that when we talk about increasing food production to feed the starving millions, everyone just nods as if it makes perfect sense.

Daniel. Didn't it make sense to you?

Elaine. Yes, I guess I have to say it did.

Daniel. Then where's the puzzle?

Elaine. To be honest, I'm not quite sure.

Daniel. Or perhaps you're not quite ready to articulate it.

Elaine. Yes, it could be that.

Daniel. Let's move on to something simpler . . . In *Ishmael* I distinguished our tribal ancestors and their present-day cultural descendants from ourselves —

Elaine. You called them Leavers and us Takers.

Daniel. Yes . . . If I were doing it again, I wouldn't have used those terms.

Elaine. Why is that?

Daniel. Because far too many readers translated these terms into Good People and Bad People. People imagined that if their hearts were in the right place, they had become Leavers. Someone once wrote to me that Governor Jerry Brown of California was a Leaver and his opponent was a Taker.

Elaine. I noticed that you don't seem to be using the terms now.

Daniel. No . . . In *Ishmael* it was simpler to say "Leavers" than "our tribal ancestors and their present-day cultural descendants," but I wish now that I'd just settled for "tribal peoples."

Elaine. I see. All the same, it did serve a purpose, at least for me.

Daniel. Go on.

Elaine. It distinguished "them" from "us" in a very . . . fundamental way. Leavers are those who leave their lives in the hands of the gods, and Takers are those who take their lives into their own hands. Leavers didn't worry about where their next meal was coming from, because they knew that the food the gods left for them was never going to go away. But that wasn't good enough for the Takers. They wanted to take control of their own food supply and not depend on the generosity of the gods.

Daniel. Yes, the names themselves were apt enough, but many readers tended to read them as *character* descriptors. The essential difference between "them" and "us" is not in our hearts or in our attitudes but in the way we live.

Elaine. Yes, I know that.

Daniel. As I described them, tribal peoples — or Leavers — live in the hands of the gods, meaning that they take what the gods send. In good times they live well and have an easy time of it. In bad times they live less well and have to put more effort into staying alive. But there was never any necessity to sit in one spot and starve to death. If there wasn't much food right where they were, they went somewhere else, where was likely to be more, and it was all free for the taking. Famines occur among settled, agricultural peoples. They're stuck in their own stricken area and can't forage for food in their neighbors' territories, because the food there is definitely not free for the taking.

Elaine. Yes, I see.

Daniel. But we're getting off the track here. I'm not trying to recapitulate what I've already written. I just needed to lay the basis for one question I received that I wanted you to take a crack at.

Elaine. Okay.

Daniel. A woman wrote that, on the basis of what I'd written about living in the hands of the gods, did I justify the practice of medicine and if so, how.

Elaine. Uh-huh.

Daniel. So, thinking like a Martian anthropologist, how do you answer this question?

Elaine [after some thought]. It seems like an instance of translating a description into a prescription.

Daniel. In other words, because Leavers lived their lives in the hands of the gods, so should we.

Elaine. That's right.

Daniel. This is a valid reply up to a certain point, but it also suggests that no description should be taken as a prescription. Are you familiar with Jean Liedloff's *Continuum Concept?*

Elaine. No.

Daniel. Jean Liedloff, an American writer, spent the early 1970s living with the Yekuana and Sanema tribes of South America, finding them to be the happiest people she'd ever known. This led her to pay particular attention to the way they reared their children. What she saw, among other things, was that their children enjoyed constant physical contact with their mothers from birth, slept in their parents' bed until leaving of their own volition, usually after about two years. She saw that they were breast-fed instantly whenever they were hungry and during infancy were in constant contact with their mothers as they went about their business. There's a great deal more to it than this, but this gives you the general idea. As a result — or at least so it seemed to Jean — children matured feeling completely secure, happy, and unneurotic. This was a description that tens of thousands — or it may be hundreds of thousands by now — have found to be a very successful prescription for child rearing. I've been around children raised this way, and I can tell you that the difference between them and children raised the usual way is striking. So you can't automatically dismiss the utility of turning a description into a prescription.

Elaine. Okay. But living in the hands of the gods . . .

Daniel. Keep in mind that this is just an expression. If you were to ask the members of an aboriginal tribe if they were living in the hands of the gods, they wouldn't know what you were talking about it, and if you explained it to them, they'd probably say, "Well, we never thought about it that way, but I guess you could say so."

Elaine. I don't think I quite understand.

Daniel. "Living in the hands of the gods" is just an expression. You could say "casting your fate to the winds" or even "trying your luck." An example will help. Every year tens of thousands of young people dream of becoming successful actors, but only a few of them actually go off to New York or Hollywood to try their luck. While this handful take acting lessons and go to auditions, they take any kind of work they can get. I say they're trying their luck, but it would be equally valid to say that they're living in the hands of the gods. Or you could say that what happens to them is up to the fates. Obviously they don't all make it; only a very few make it. But if these few hadn't put themselves in the hands of the gods — hadn't left home to scuffle for work and face a lot of hardship and rejection — they wouldn't have made it at all. No one who stays home and plays it safe becomes a success on the stage or screen.

Elaine. Yes, I can see that.

Daniel. Most people in our culture strive for a maximum of control over their destiny — avoid at all costs anything that looks like living in the hands of the gods. This often assures a certain success, but it almost never brings a lightning strike of good fortune. They get along, according to plan, they advance toward collecting their retirement benefits, but that's it. Lightning strikes only those who are willing to risk living in the hands of the gods.

Elaine. And — if I may ask — how does this translate into your own life?

Daniel. You may definitely ask. For the first twenty years of my life I followed the conventional trajectory, in control as much as possible at every point. I had a career in publishing and over a twenty-year period moved steadily upward. In my last position I just had to hold on and keep my head down, and a vice presidency would have been mine almost certainly — and, ultimately, quite possibly the presidency of the company I was working for. Instead I walked away from it. I won't say I had no plans at that point, but they were terrible plans, and within a couple of years you could say pretty safely that I had nothing. And having nothing, I started writing a book, and with a little help from the gods or the fates or the universe, I was able to keep working on that book for twelve years until it became *Ishmael.* And just at that point, with a little more help from the gods or the fates or the universe, it so happened that Ted Turner decided he wanted to sponsor a competition for a novel presenting "creative and positive solutions to global problems." Winning that competition assured the publication of *Ishmael* — and there was my lightning strike. But back in 1975, if I'd held on and kept my head down and finally made it to the top in publishing, there would've been no *Ishmael* — or any of the subsequent books. I had to let go of my life for that to happen.

Elaine. That's quite a story. And quite an example.

Daniel. I should point out, however, that during this period it would never have occurred to me that I was "living in the hands of the gods." I was, but it wasn't something I consciously set out to do.

Elaine. I see.

Daniel. So finally we get to the reader's question. Doesn't the practice of medicine somehow violate the principle of living in the hands of the gods?

Elaine [after some thought]. It would seem to.

Daniel. So it seemed, at least to this reader. Is that the answer you'd expect me to give her?

Elaine. No.

Daniel. Then what?

Elaine [laughing]. I don't know.

Daniel. You've got to pull back to get a wider perspective on the question. That's the job of the Martian anthropologist: to pull back, never to be restricted to the questioner's assumptions.

Elaine shakes her head.

Daniel. This reader was fixated on a detail and not looking at the whole.

Elaine. The whole *what?*

Daniel. You know the whole. The difference between you and her is that I'm pressuring you to look at it.

Elaine [after a minute]. Aboriginal peoples practiced — still practice — their own kind of medicine.

Daniel. That's certainly true. Do you think it's like ours?

Elaine. I can't claim to know what it is, but . . . But I suppose I have an impression that it's more like magic than anything we'd consider medicine.

Daniel. So how does this help answer this woman's question?

Elaine. I'm not sure it does.

Daniel. What do you think is troubling this woman about our medicine? Why does she think it doesn't jibe with living in the hands of the gods?

Elaine [sighing]. I guess she's thinking . . . "Oh well, I've got pneumonia. For someone living in the hands of the gods, that's it."

Daniel. You live with it — or die with it.

Elaine. If you're living in the hands of the gods.

Daniel [after some thought]. What causes pneumonia?

Elaine. I think it can be caused either by bacteria or viruses.

Daniel. And what would a modern doctor's treatment be?

Elaine. I assume the treatment would be to attack the bacteria or virus, probably with antibiotics.

Daniel. And this attack — do you think this is what's bothering this reader? All the attacks that medicine provides against the hosts of organisms that are hostile to human life?

Elaine. That sounds like a good guess.

Daniel. Tell me what's going on in her mind. That's part of the anthropologist's job, to understand what's going on in the minds of his subjects. See if you can speak her thoughts.

Elaine. Wow. Let's see. I think it's something like this. "In general, Leaver peoples live at peace with the world. They've got plenty of competitors in the world. Other animals compete for the game, but they don't hunt down these animals to wipe them out. They've got competitors for everything they eat, but they don't try to wipe them out."

Daniel. Whereas we Takers do. As far as possible, we wipe out the wolves and the foxes and the coyotes that prey on our livestock. As far as possible, we try to wipe out all the creatures that feed on our crops.

Elaine. We're at war with the world of life around us.

Daniel. So maybe medicine is part of the same war.

Elaine. Yes, that's it.

Daniel. That's what's troubling this reader.

Elaine. I think so.

Daniel. Does it trouble you? Are you going to refuse treatment if you get pneumonia?

Elaine. No, I'm afraid not.

Daniel. You think maybe you should, but you won't.

Elaine. Something like that.

Daniel. You're still trapped in this woman's circle of thought. You have to pull back farther and see the whole.

Elaine shakes her head, discouraged.

Daniel. Let's call it a day. See if you can use the rest of the day to figure out how to pull back far enough to see the answer we're looking for.

Elaine. Okay.

Daniel. Try jumping the track this woman's question has you on. She's presented you with some lined paper. Stop trying to write on the next line provided. Turn the paper sideways.

Elaine. What is the track?

Daniel. Think about it. I'm sure you can answer that yourself. *[After some thought.]* It occurs to me that this may help. *[Changing the subject.]* You understand that this is a process of discovery for me as well. I'm trying to figure out and articulate what I do when presented with a question like this one — or any question.

Elaine. Yes . . . ?

Daniel. This woman was unable to answer her own question because she's wearing blinders. I'm not sure if horses on the street still wear blinders, but you know what they are.

Elaine. They're . . . objects . . . I suppose squares of leather . . . put at the side of a horse's head to keep its eyes on the path ahead.

Daniel. To block out distracting things it might see if it had a wider view of its surroundings.

Elaine. Exactly.

Daniel. Most people, in trying to deal with this woman's question, will adopt her blinders, will keep their eyes on the path she sees and agree to block out any wider view of the matter.

Elaine. Yes, I see that.

Daniel. So your job tonight is to take off the blinders and see what else there is to think about. This is another — and probably better — way of talking about jumping the track she has us on. We can't see another track to jump to until we take off the blinders she's offered us to wear.

Elaine. Got it.

Friday: Morning

Daniel. So. Any progress?

Elaine. I think so.

Daniel. Did you figure out what track this reader had us on, wearing her blinders?

Elaine. The track was medicine.

Daniel. As possibly in conflict with the notion of living in the hands of the gods. And what happened when you took off the blinders she provided for you?

Elaine. I saw everything else.

Daniel. You were able to pull back and achieve a wider vision than she has.

Elaine. That's right.

Daniel. Go ahead.

Elaine. What I saw was that disease — or at least most diseases — represent an attack by other living creatures. What I saw was that every creature has a right to defend itself from attack any way it can, and that includes us.

Daniel. Attacked by a lion, we're going to use any weapon that's available to defend ourselves.

Elaine. That's right. And medicine provides us with weapons with which to defend ourselves against viruses and bacteria, among other things.

Daniel. And living in the hands of the gods?

Elaine. Living in the hands of the gods has nothing to do with it. Living in the hands of the gods doesn't mean standing there and letting the lion rip your head off.

Daniel. Well done. What do you think? Was it hard to get to the answer?

Elaine [ponders this for a bit]. I guess I have to say it was . . . Maybe it's like learning to ride a bicycle. At first it seems completely impossible, then somehow, suddenly, you've got it.

Daniel. Yes. Of course, being able to move forward without falling down is just the basic skill, the beginning of confidence that leads to more advanced feats.

Elaine. Of course . . . I have a question of my own. It's probably been asked many times.

Daniel. Go ahead.

Elaine. We've been talking about living in the hands of the gods.

Daniel. Yes?

Elaine. But you never make it quite clear whether you *believe* in these gods, or any god.

Daniel. When Ishmael talks about the gods . . . Let me start that a different way. The subject of *Ishmael* is the unrecognized and unacknowledged mythology of our culture, which Ishmael formulates as a story that spells out the relationships among Man, the world, and the gods. In this context the gods are mythological, which is not to say that they're unreal but rather that their reality is irrelevant. The world was made for Man to conquer and rule, and Man was made to conquer and rule it — according to our mythology. It goes without saying that this is a divinely appointed mission. The Europeans who drove the Indians off their lands and put that land to the plow sincerely believed they were doing God's work.

Elaine. Yes, I understand that. But I don't see how it answers my question.

Daniel. Which is, do I believe in God.

Elaine. Yes, I guess so.

Daniel. Being a Martian anthropologist, I have to pull back from your question, have to take off the blinders you're asking me to wear. Believing in things that may not exist — or disbelieving in things that *may* exist — is a peculiarity of your culture, not a universal human activity. Because it's universal among you, you assume it's universal among humans in general.

Elaine. That's true. It never occurred to me that it might not be universal among humans.

Daniel. You variously believe in God, though God may not exist, or you disbelieve in God, though God may exist. You variously believe in angels, though angels may not exist, or you disbelieve in angels, though angels may exist. You variously believe in extraterrestrial spacecraft that have the world under surveillance, though these spacecraft may not exist, or disbelieve in them, though they may exist. You variously believe in ghosts, though ghosts may not exist, or you disbelieve in ghosts, though ghosts may exist.

Elaine. Yes, that's all true.

Daniel. Tell me, do you believe in supermodels?

Elaine [laughing]. Supermodels? I don't *believe* in them. That isn't the word I would use.

Daniel. For you, the existence of supermodels doesn't require you to exercise the faculty of belief.

Elaine. That's true. Though I've never thought of belief as a faculty.

Daniel. Oh, it definitely is. It's the faculty you must call upon in the face of the absurd. As William of Occam put it, *Credo quia absurdum*: "I believe because it is absurd." A thing whose reality doesn't seem to you absurd doesn't require belief.

Elaine. Yes, I suppose that's true. But the existence of God doesn't strike me as absurd.

Daniel. It's absurd in the sense that no one can produce even the slightest evidence of God's existence. They can produce *proofs*, but these are only valid if you accept the premises on which they're based. If you don't accept those premises, then they're just empty exercises in logic.

Elaine. I suppose I'm dimly aware that such things exist.

Daniel. Another faculty exists that is a kind of cousin of the faculty of belief. This is the faculty that comes into play with regard to supermodels. You *people the world* with supermodels. Fifty years ago there were no supermodels, but in the last few decades you have peopled your world with them. A hundred

years ago there were no movie stars, but since then you've
peopled your world with hundreds of them. Europe in the
Middle Ages was peopled with saints.

Elaine. Yes, I see what you mean.

Daniel. The Gebusi of New Guinea consort with spirits on a
daily basis. Their world is peopled with spirits, and if you were
to ask them if they *believe* in spirits, they would react just the
way you did when I asked you if you believe in supermodels . . .
But to return to your original question, I have to say that the
faculty of belief is completely atrophied in me. It strikes me as
foolish to believe in things that may not exist — or to deny the
existence of things that may exist. Nonetheless, I've peopled my
own personal universe with gods who have a care for all living
things. I don't pray to these gods or build shrines to them or
expect favors from them or perform rituals for them. Nor do I
expect other people to "believe" in these gods or to people their
own universes with them.

Elaine. I understand. This resolves a question that was very
much on my mind — and is probably on the minds of many of
your readers.

Daniel. What question is that?

Elaine. I imagine a great many of your readers consider you a
nonbeliever.

Daniel. I assume you mean a nonbeliever in the Judeo-
Christian God.

Elaine. In any kind of god.

Daniel. I'm afraid I don't know whether that's true or not. But
I'm not sure why this is relevant. Or what question I've resolved
for you.

Elaine. You've explained how it was possible for you to write a book like *Tales of Adam*, in which the gods figure so prominently.

Daniel. Yes . . . ?

Elaine. Some readers must wonder if you were writing from the heart or if it was just a sort of . . . poetic re-creation of the animist worldview.

Daniel. Someone might imagine that I'd merely adopted an animist persona — a false or alien persona — for literary purposes, as James Hogg did in writing his *Confessions of a Justified Sinner.*

Elaine. I'm afraid I'm not familiar with that.

Daniel. It's a classic that enjoys a sort of cult status. To write it, Hogg had to adopt a persona diametrically opposed to his own, that of an extreme predestinarian, one who believes that one's salvation or damnation was ordained unalterably by God from the beginning of time. Believing himself to be of the elect, regardless of any sin he might commit, the narrator considered himself "justified" even as he murdered his brother, his mother, and others, and allowed others to be hanged for his crimes. The book, written in the early 1820s, decades ahead of its time, was received with scorn and fell into obscurity until being rediscovered by authors like Robert Louis Stevenson and André Gide . . . In any case, you can be sure that the *Tales* were definitely written "from my heart," to use your phrase.

Elaine. I didn't doubt it.

Daniel. So . . . Where are we? I take it we've disposed of the question of my personal beliefs.

Elaine. Yes.

Daniel. Let's see . . . On the same general subject, how would you answer this question, which I've received in many different forms: "Do you think God recognizes the danger we pose to the world and therefore sends such things as AIDS, cancer, plagues, and natural disasters to keep our population in check?"

Elaine [after thinking about it]. It strikes me as a pretty silly question.

Daniel. Yes, perhaps it is. But when an anthropologist sees people doing or saying something that seems silly, he asks himself two questions: "Why does this seem silly to me?" and "Why doesn't it seem silly to *them*?"

Elaine. Yes. Of course you're right.

Daniel. So why does the question seem silly to you?

Elaine. Perhaps it would seem less silly if it weren't a question about God.

Daniel. You'll have to explain that. Is asking questions about God inherently silly or do you find the very concept of God silly?

Elaine. No, neither one . . . Would you repeat the question?

Daniel. "Do you think God recognizes the danger we pose to the world and therefore sends such things as AIDS, cancer, plagues, and natural disasters to keep our population in check?"

Elaine [after thinking for several minutes]. The questioner doesn't seem to realize that there is any causality at work in the world except divine causality. He uses the term *natural disasters* but doesn't actually accept the fact that they *are* natural. He doesn't connect the tsunami that devastated South Asia with an undersea earthquake, he thinks God "sent" it.

Daniel. Or "sent" the earthquake.

Elaine. AIDS, cancer, plagues — all these things have natural causes.

Daniel. Yes, that's what you and I and probably most people think, but you need to get inside this person's head and understand his vision of God.

Elaine. His vision of God . . . I'm not sure what to say.

Daniel. Talk about his God.

Elaine [after some thought]. His God is, I'd have to assume, omniscient and omnipotent.

Daniel. I'm sure you're right. Go on.

Elaine. I don't see where to go.

Daniel. I'm trying not to lead you too pointedly. You have to get behind the thought processes that prompted this question. You have an omniscient and omnipotent God, and . . .

Elaine. He sees that we're overpopulating the world.

Daniel. And . . .

Elaine. And it's within his power to send diseases and catastrophes to reduce our population.

Daniel. Why does he need to do this?

Elaine. Ah. Because the world doesn't regulate itself. Or you could say that God can't depend on the world to regulate itself.

Daniel. And because the world doesn't regulate itself — or can't be depended on to regulate itself...

Elaine. God has to do it himself. He has to manage the world personally.

Daniel. Otherwise it doesn't work properly. At least not automatically.

Elaine. Right.

Daniel. So he sends diseases and catastrophes in order to reduce the human population. Or at least he has the option and the power to do this.

Elaine. That's right.

Daniel. But...

Elaine. But?

Daniel. He has the option and the power to reduce the human population by all sorts of means, but...

Elaine. He can't manage to do it.

Daniel. So he created a world that can't be counted on to regulate itself and that he can't seem to regulate, either. What kind of a God is this?

Elaine. What *kind*? According to who?

Daniel. According to the person who asked this question.

Elaine. I don't know, beyond the obvious — beyond the things we've already discussed... I mean, he's omniscient and omnipotent. I suppose I could add that he's benevolent. That he exerts himself on our behalf — or may be doing so.

Daniel. As always, I'm trying to get behind the words, back to unvoiced assumptions and beliefs.

Elaine sighs.

Daniel [after giving her a couple of minutes to think]. Let's give God a performance review, starting with the Garden of Eden, where he planted a tree whose fruit Adam and Eve were forbidden to taste. Put yourself in his place in an analogous situation. You're the mother of two children, a boy and a girl. You tell them, "You can play with anything in the house except the loaded gun I'm putting here on the kitchen table." Then, as you leave, you knowingly allow someone into the house who will undoubtedly encourage them to play with the gun.

Elaine. Uh-huh. But a believer would say that God put the forbidden tree in the garden as a test.

Daniel. And being omniscient . . .

Elaine. He'd know they would fail it.

Daniel. Even a human mother would know better than to leave her children with a loaded gun in plain sight, wouldn't she?

Elaine. Yes.

Daniel. I don't know what sort of religious upbringing you had.

Elaine. Oh, I was raised a Catholic. Went to a Catholic grade school, had the Bible stories, learned the catechism, and all that.

Daniel. Then you're in a pretty good position to evaluate God's performance. His early experiences with the human race were pretty disappointing.

Elaine. Yes. He finally became so disgusted that he wiped it all out except for Noah and his family. Even the results of this weren't too satisfactory.

Daniel. Eventually he decided to adopt a chosen people to be his own. What was his thought in doing this?

Elaine. Hmm. I'm a bit hazy on that one. I mean, on his long-term plan for the race as a whole. But the idea in the short term was to champion this one people and help them surpass all their neighbors, as long as they remained faithful to him.

Daniel. And how did that work out?

Elaine. Not too well. In the end they were so faithless that he washed his hands of them. Allowed them to be overrun first by their neighbors, then by the Romans. At least this is the way I remember it.

Daniel. But he nonetheless promised them a Messiah.

Elaine. That's right.

Daniel. And this Messiah would do what?

Elaine. I'm not exactly sure what was promised, but the Jews assumed the Messiah would restore their independence and put them back at the pinnacle of the human race.

Daniel. And did he send them their Messiah?

Elaine. Well, obviously opinions differ on that. The Jews didn't think Jesus was the Messiah, and still don't. Certainly he didn't do what they'd expected of a Messiah.

Daniel. But Jesus *was* the Messiah, wasn't he?

Elaine. According to Christians, yes.

Daniel. According to Christians, he was the Messiah not merely of the Jews but of the whole human race.

Elaine. That's right. Presumably.

Daniel. But only Christians got this message. The Jews are still waiting, and the Muslims consider Jesus to be just another prophet.

Elaine. Yes, that's true.

Daniel. If Jesus was sent to save the entire human race, why is it that only Christians got this message?

Elaine. That I don't know.

Daniel. If you were an omnipotent God, do you think you could have managed to get this message across to the whole human race? One way or the other — that Jesus either was or was not the promised Messiah.

Elaine. I think so.

Daniel. Naturally, Christians believe that they got the message God intended to send. But what's ultimately happened to Christianity?

Elaine. Ultimately? I'm not sure what you mean. It's still here.

Daniel. But very different from what it was a thousand years ago.

Elaine. That's true. It's become splintered into a thousand different sects, each with its own version of the message.

Daniel. They disagree on all sorts of vital issues: divorce, birth control, abortion, homosexuality. Not to mention the primacy of the pope and even the means of salvation.

Elaine. True.

Daniel. If you were an omnipotent God, don't you think you could have made yourself absolutely clear on these issues?

Elaine. Yes, I think I could have.

Daniel. So I ask again: What kind of God is this?

Elaine [after some thought]. Strangely enough, I would have to say that he's an incompetent God. Which is . . .

Daniel. Yes?

Elaine. I suppose God has been called every bad name you can think of for a ruler — tyrannical, vengeful, merciless, indifferent to our sufferings, obsessed with rules and regulations, a spy who peeks into every bedroom — but I don't think I've ever heard him called incompetent.

Daniel. This is my career, uncovering the *unvoiced* beliefs and assumptions of our culture. For example, it's the *unvoiced* belief of our culture that the world is a human possession, that it was our divinely appointed destiny to conquer and rule it, that ours is the one *right* way for humans to live, and that we must cling to this way of life even if it kills us. And it is the unvoiced assumption of this questioner that God is incompetent.

Elaine. You'll have to explain that.

Daniel. Consider the inadequate means this questioner suggests that God might be using to reduce our population: AIDS, plagues, natural disasters, and so on. Our population continues to grow steadily despite such things, and has done so steadily for the past ten thousand years despite such things. If he was competent — and really concerned — an omnipotent God would be able to do something really effective, wouldn't he?

Elaine. I'd have to think so. Though it would be, would have to be . . .

Daniel [*after a few moments*]. What sort of thing are you thinking of?

Elaine. A vast famine . . . a plague like none we've ever seen.

Daniel. You can be more imaginative than that, even if you've just had a few moments to think about it. Think of something that wouldn't cause a single death, either of plague or starvation.

Elaine [*after some thought*]. He could strike ninety-nine out of every hundred women barren.

Daniel. Of course. That would take care of the problem in a hurry, wouldn't it. In a single generation, our population would drop from six billion to sixty million, without anyone dying of plague or starving to death.

Elaine. Yes.

Daniel. If you're clever enough to come up with that solution in sixty seconds, shouldn't an omniscient and omnipotent God be able to do as well?

Elaine. You would think so. Though I don't know what a believer would say to such a proposition.

Daniel. Believers are generally reconciled to the idea that God no longer intervenes in human affairs the way he once did. We're on our own. He sent Jesus to open the gates of heaven to fallen humanity, and we'll have to be content with that.

Elaine. Yes, apparently.

Daniel. Though our questioner doesn't subscribe to this notion. He thinks God may be making efforts to save us from ourselves, even if those efforts are ineffective . . . But you see now why this person doesn't think his question is silly.

Elaine. Yes. He's reconciled to the fact that his God is incompetent. God *wants* to intervene and *may be* intervening, but the guy asking this question isn't surprised that God's interventions are so obviously . . . feeble.

Daniel. In fact, the real gods of the world — if there are any — are competent gods. They created a world that functions perfectly, without divine oversight or intervention. If we don't curb our population growth, the built-in processes of the world will take care of it. If we continue to attack them as vigorously as we are right now, the ecological systems that keep us alive will eventually collapse, leaving a world that won't sustain human life at all. We'll be gone — probably along with most or all large forms of animal life — but life will go on and start rebuilding anew, just as it's done after every mass extinction of the past.

Elaine. Not a happy outcome. At least from our point of view.

Daniel. But also not a necessary outcome. The people of the world simply must confront the fact that the period of mass extinctions that will end with our own has already begun, and that this isn't something we can just go on ignoring.

Elaine. Yes.

Daniel. So what has exploring this silly question taught you?

Elaine. A great deal more than I expected, obviously.

Daniel. I mean about . . . What I'm trying to convey to you is the way I come up with answers that confound people's expectations. What I'm trying to develop here is the answer to the last big remaining question that people have for me: How do I do what I do?

Elaine. I'll have to think about that.

Daniel. Okay. Let's take a break.

Daniel [half an hour later]. So did you give any thought to my last question?

Elaine. I gave some thought to it, but all I can really say is that I'm not even close to being able to do what you do.

Daniel. With the last question we explored, I really only had to give you a helping hand at one point, when I asked you what kind of God this questioner was thinking of.

Elaine. True. *[After giving the matter some thought.]* But that was the *critical* point. If you hadn't stepped in to give me some guidance, I don't think I could've gotten there on my own.

Daniel. It's early days yet. You said it was like learning how to ride a bike. Just knowing how to stay upright is only the beginning. It takes some practice to get to a point where you can pedal with no hands.

Elaine. True.

Daniel. Here's a question one of my readers couldn't unravel, but I'll bet that by now you won't find it much of a challenge. He wrote that, when the six billionth person was born back in 1999, a writer for the *National Review* tried to put it into perspective by pointing out that if all six billion of us lived in Texas, each of us would have an eighth of an acre to ourselves. My correspondent asked, "This doesn't seem like that much of a problem to me, does it to you?"

Elaine. Uh-huh.

Daniel. Just "uh-huh"?

Elaine. Well, I assume the arithmetic is correct.

Daniel. I assume so, too. Though I suspect the author of the article was working with Texas's total area, not with its total *living* area, which wouldn't include rivers, lakes, streets, and highways.

Elaine. I'm a little vague about how big an acre really is.

Daniel. I anticipated the question. An acre is 43,560 square feet. An eighth of an acre is 5,445 square feet, about the size of an ordinary city building lot. A family of four would have half an acre, a common size for suburban lots.

Elaine. Okay.

Daniel. Plenty of room.

Elaine. Yes.

Daniel. So now you have our population situation in perspective.

Elaine says nothing.

Daniel. Come on, Elaine. What's the unvoiced assumption behind this "perspective"?

Elaine. Obviously it's about space.

Daniel. Work it through. This is an easy one.

Elaine [after thinking about it]. A family of four has no trouble living on half an acre. Millions of Americans do it.

Daniel. I'm not going to help you with this one. Think about what you're saying, word by word.

Elaine [after thinking some more]. All right. They're living *on* half an acre, but they're not living *off* half an acre.

Daniel. Of course not. What would happen if they *tried* to live off half an acre?

Elaine. My guess is, they couldn't.

Daniel. Of course they couldn't. So now put the idea of six billion people living in Texas into perspective.

Elaine. They would have to be importing vast amounts of food.

Daniel says nothing.

Elaine [after a couple of minutes of thought]. There'd be no one out there to import any food *from*. All the farms in the rest of the world would be untenanted. Nobody outside Texas would be growing food, harvesting it, processing and packaging it, transporting it.

Daniel. Bravo . . . I did a little research during our break. Roughly speaking, a square mile of farmland will feed about a thousand people. If all the land in Texas were completely deforested and put under cultivation, it would feed about 262 million people. So . . . ?

Elaine. So the six billion people in Texas wouldn't be *living* there, they'd be *starving* there.

Daniel. But they'd have plenty of room for houses, patios, swing sets, and swimming pools.

Elaine. Yes. That's what the writer in the *National Review* had in mind.

Daniel. To be honest, I was surprised that you were initially so ready to accept this vision as plausible.

Elaine. Why? It must have been plausible to everyone at the *National Review* — and to its readers.

Daniel. True, but consider the original question I presented you with. The questioner said, "This makes sense to me, doesn't it make sense to you?" You must have known my answer was going to be "No, it doesn't make sense to me."

Elaine. I suppose I did. *[Thinks for a bit.]* But that doesn't change the fact that it did make sense to *me*. At that point.

Daniel. If you're going to learn to think like a Martian anthro-pologist, you're going to have to become far more suspicious of the reasonable-sounding propositions that we're constantly being presented with. Like this one, pointing out that there's enough land in Texas to accommodate the whole world's population in comfort. I'm sure that tens of thousands accepted this statement without blinking an eye, and that millions more would accept it the same way if it were presented to them.

Elaine. I'm sure you're right.

Daniel. In effect, I'm trying to break you of the habit of auto-matically saying, "Yes, this makes sense. I'll accept it." I'm trying to train you to pause and say, "Yes, this *seems* to make sense. But does it?"

Elaine [after some thought]. I can say that I understand what you're saying, but I'm not really sure I do. I mean . . . we're trained to pause when something *doesn't* make sense. But when something *does* make sense . . . ? You surely don't pause every single time something makes sense.

Daniel. You're right, of course.

Elaine. So it's a matter of knowing *when* to pause, isn't it? How do *you* know when to pause?

Daniel. That's a very valid question. A very useful and helpful one, in fact.

Elaine. Why helpful?

Daniel. It points me in a direction I hadn't seen, hadn't prepared myself to explore with you. Let me see if I can explain . . . If you were to follow an aboriginal hunter through the forest, he'd see things that were literally invisible to you. He'd see and recognize marks in the dirt that you'd have to concentrate to see at all. He'd notice disturbances in the grass that would be imperceptible to you.

Elaine. I'm sure that's true.

Daniel. The same would be true for the hunter if he were to follow you through the women's section of a department store. You'd immediately distinguish between the really good clothes and the cheap ones, which he certainly wouldn't. You'd notice a clerk having a personal conversation on the phone. Without even thinking about it, you'd be aware of the subtle differences between a personal telephone conversation and a business conversation, and the hunter wouldn't.

Elaine. True.

Daniel. What we see are the things our circumstances have trained us to pay attention to. Your circumstances don't require you to notice slight marks in the dust. The hunter's circumstances don't require him to notice the difference between beautifully made garments and poorly made ones.

Elaine. True.

Daniel. I've trained myself to recognize the voice of Mother Culture in the things I read and hear. You know what I mean by Mother Culture.

Elaine. Yes. Mother Culture is . . . the *personification* of all the collective wisdom that comes to us from our parents, our schoolteachers, our textbooks, our movies, our television commentators . . .

Daniel. And our magazines, including *Scientific American* and the *National Review.*

Elaine. Right.

Daniel. I recognized Mother Culture's voice immediately in the *National Review* observation that the whole world's population could be accommodated comfortably within the boundaries of Texas. Do you see why?

Elaine. I'm not sure.

Daniel. Take a stab at it.

Elaine [*after some thought*]. Mother Culture wants to reassure us that everything we're doing is okay. Reaching a population of six billion is nothing to be worried about.

Daniel. Because, look, you could fit all six billion of us inside Texas with room to spare. I recognized it instantly as the kind of reassurance Mother Culture wants us to have. That's what made me pause to examine it. And once I started examining it, it took me only a few moments to identify its absurdity.

Elaine. Okay. But I can't really say that this does me much good. You say that you've trained yourself to recognize the voice of Mother Culture in the things you read or hear, but how does this help *me?*

Daniel [*after thinking about this for a minute*]. I guess you could say that what the hunter is looking for as he moves through the forest are tip-offs, things that signal what's going on around him. When you examine a shirt or a dress, there are probably things that tip you off as to its quality.

Elaine. Yes, I guess so.

Daniel. I'm looking for tip-offs as well. Or, as I say, I've trained myself to notice them. I don't have to look for them, they leap out at me.

Elaine. But what are they?

Daniel. I can't give you a list — it's never occurred to me to make one. Maybe we'll be able to compile one as we go along.

Elaine. What was the tip-off in this case?

Daniel [*after some thought*]. Its obvious tendentiousness. I mean by this that the statement clearly contains an implicit argument. If someone says that if you lined up all the cars in the world on a single highway, it would encircle the globe twice, there is no implicit argument. He's just presenting you with an interesting fact. He's not saying that this is something that could actually be done. He's not making any special point about cars, highways, or the circumference of the earth. He's just using his computational skills to give us a visual image of how many cars we have. The writer who says Texas could comfortably accommodate six billion people *does* have a point, and he *is* saying that it could be done.

Elaine. Okay. But I'm not sure I'd recognize a tendentious statement if I saw one.

Daniel. Of course you would. Let me see if I can think of a couple . . . Here's one from, I believe, a French military man of the seventeenth century: "God is generally on the side of the big battalions against the small ones."

Elaine. Uh-huh.

Daniel. I'm sure you can see what implicit point of view this statement expresses.

Elaine. Yes. He's saying that, on the battlefield, God has nothing to do with who wins and who loses.

Daniel. Of course. Let me think for a bit . . . Pope John Paul the Second said, "Vast sections of society are confused about what is right and what is wrong." Implicit in this statement is . . . ?

Elaine. That *he* isn't confused about it.

Daniel. Of course . . . From the beginning, I've been saying that our job is to look behind the words people give us in order to understand the implicit notions that are generating them.

Elaine. Yes, I see that — now. What are some other tip-offs?

Daniel. Things to look for are elements of the received wisdom of our culture — received without acknowledgment or examination. For example, it's received wisdom that everyone knows the difference between right and wrong. We imagine that this knowledge arises from the structure of the human mind itself. In fact, we use this as a measure of sanity in our courts. And by this measure, I would be considered insane.

Elaine laughs.

Daniel. In one of my early books — I think it was probably *Ishmael* — I made the point that missionaries were astonished to find that the aboriginal peoples they worked among didn't know right from wrong, and I said the missionaries were quite correct in their observation. I received several indignant letters about this from people who thought I was denigrating aboriginal peoples, implying that they were somehow subhuman. Whatever the missionaries thought, *of course* these peoples knew right from wrong!

Elaine. I'm not sure why you say you yourself don't know right from wrong.

Daniel. To me — as to the aborigines being evangelized — these are quite arbitrary categories that can be switched back and forth at will. For example, you know very well that abortion was very seriously wrong before *Roe v. Wade*. After *Roe v. Wade* it became right, though naturally there are still people who think it's wrong. Which is it, right or wrong?

Elaine. I think a woman has the right to choose to have an abortion.

Daniel. You mean she has the right to do something that's wrong?

Elaine. No. It isn't something wrong.

Daniel. Are you hesitant to call it right?

Elaine. No.

Daniel. But I'm sure you're aware that tens of millions of Americans would like to see *Roe v. Wade* reversed, would like to see abortion outlawed again.

Elaine. Yes.

Daniel. And if they succeeded in having the present law overturned, would abortion then be right or wrong?

Elaine has no answer.

Daniel. If you'd like to know how wrong abortion seemed to people fifty years ago, you should see a movie called *Detective Story*, based on a very successful Broadway play by Sidney Kingsley. The action takes place in a station house, where a detective played by Kirk Douglas is interrogating one of the most loathsome criminals he's ever encountered, an abortionist. Unfortunately, his zeal leads him to a horrendous discovery — his own wife was once one of the abortionist's clients. Now he sees his wife as almost as loathsome as the abortionist himself — and this revelation all but tears him apart. This was not a picture directed toward a bigoted, minority audience. It was nominated for four Academy Awards and won one.

Elaine still has nothing to say.

Daniel. If the present law were overturned, a woman would be imprisoned for having an abortion. Yes?

Elaine. That's right.

Daniel. Would her punishment be wrongful?

Elaine. Not according to the law.

Daniel. Ah, the law! So by changing a law, something that's right today can become something that's wrong tomorrow. Isn't that so?

Elaine. Yes. And of course the reverse is true as well. Something that's wrong today can become something that's right tomorrow, if the law is changed.

Daniel. Is capital punishment right or wrong?

Elaine. Some people think it's right, some people think it's wrong.

Daniel. So, collectively, do these people know right from wrong?

Elaine. Not in this instance.

Daniel. And in the instance of abortion do people collectively know right from wrong?

Elaine. No.

Daniel. Is sex between persons of the same gender right or wrong?

Elaine. Again, some people think it's right and some people think it's wrong.

Daniel. What about assisted suicide?

Elaine. The same. Some say it's right and some say it's wrong.

Daniel. What about using animals in scientific research?

Elaine. The same.

Daniel. But these are all people who would insist that they know right from wrong, aren't they?

Elaine. Yes, I'd think so.

Daniel. But in fact, for some strange reason, they can't agree on what's right and what's wrong in these and many other cases.

Elaine. They agree on it in most cases, I think. For example, they all agree that murder is wrong.

Daniel. Murder is *defined* as wrong, Elaine. Murder is *wrongful killing.* Isn't that so?

Elaine. Yes.

Daniel. But not all killing is wrongful. Killing in self-defense isn't wrongful, and it isn't murder.

Elaine. True.

Daniel. People will also agree that theft is wrong, but again, theft is *defined* as wrong. Theft is wrongful taking. Everyone can agree that acts that are *defined* as wrongful are wrong. In other words, people know right from wrong when the law tells them which is which. But the same law is subject to change. What's right today can be wrong tomorrow and vice versa.

Elaine. Yes, that's true.

Daniel. Can you understand now why those aboriginals had a hard time grasping this distinction that was so clear to the missionaries? To the missionaries it seemed completely self-evident. To the aboriginals it seemed completely arbitrary — as it does to me.

Elaine. This is an example of something you described in *Beyond Civilization.* I don't remember what you called it. The cultural . . . something or other.

Daniel. The cultural fallacy. The belief that the ideas that come to us as the received wisdom of our culture are innate to the human mind — that they actually arise from the structure of the human mind itself. According to this particular cultural fallacy, someone who can't tell the difference between right and wrong is either retarded or insane . . . This looks like a good stopping point.

Elaine. I have a question.

Daniel. Okay.

Elaine. In your writings on the food race, and I think in "The New Renaissance," you talk about the fact that we're attacking the biodiversity of this planet by systematically converting the biomass of other species into human mass.

Daniel. Yes?

Elaine. Isn't that something you would consider wrong?

Daniel. You haven't quite gotten my point here. I'm not interested in sorting things out into these categories, right and wrong. In other words, my point is not that what we're doing here is *wrong* but that it's unsustainable. It's undermining the human future on this planet, and I'm not going to quibble over whether this is to be categorized as right or wrong. I don't give a damn which it is.

Elaine. Okay. You're right. I hadn't quite gotten your point about this. I think I see it now . . . While we're right here, I have another question, or maybe it's just an observation.

Daniel. Go ahead.

Elaine. It seems to me that the most astounding single sentence in all your work is "There is no one right way for people to live." But I have the feeling this just floats over most people's heads.

Daniel. It does seem that way, which surprises me. It certainly hasn't aroused any great controversy that I'm aware of, though I've had a few questions about it. One reader wrote, "I think I know of one right way for people to live, and that's letting everyone live the way they want to live." How would you reply to that?

Elaine [after some thought]. I don't know.

Daniel. Think about it over lunch. You have a tendency . . . This question comes from a certain frame of reference. You can't just accept that frame of reference without challenge. Put yourself in this person's mind and dig into his words. Then pull back away from it and see if it makes sense . . . It's like a negotiation, and this is his first offer: "I know of one right way for people to live, and that's letting everyone live the way they want to live." If you look closely at the terms of his offer, you'll see why it has to be rejected. What he's saying is nonsense. You have to formulate a counteroffer in your own terms, from your own frame of reference, then you'll have your reply.

Friday: Afternoon

Daniel. So. What did you come up with?

Elaine. Nothing, I'm afraid. I really don't see how to argue with what he's saying.

Daniel [after some thought]. I've been thinking about your difficulties in a general way, and I hope that you won't be offended by my conclusion. It's certainly not an observation original to me that women in our society are generally expected to get along by being acquiescent, whereas men are expected to be assertive.

Elaine. That's certainly true.

Daniel. The reason you don't see how to argue with this person's proposition is that you've begun by acquiescing to it, by saying, "Yes, you seem to be making a lot of sense."

Elaine. I guess that's true. I see his point, and I see some validity to it.

Daniel. If we're going to make any progress here, I'm afraid you're going to have to resist the long-standing impulse to listen, nod, and acquiesce.

Elaine. A lifetime in the schools will do that to you.

Daniel. I understand completely, but it's time to begin fighting the impulse.

Elaine. I know. I'll do my best.

Daniel. In this case, what you have to do is turn the tables on this person. You understand the expression?

Elaine. Turn the tables? Yes, of course.

Daniel. What are "the tables"?

Elaine. Oh. Well. That I don't know specifically.

Daniel. Do you play chess?

Elaine. Yes.

Daniel. Turning the tables is the most aggressive chess move of all. If you're playing the black pieces and you see that your opponent has developed a winning position, you turn the table around so that you're now playing the white pieces and he's playing the black. You've usurped what appears to be his superior position.

Elaine. Hardly a legal move.

Daniel. No, but it's the origin of the expression. Right now the person who has made this statement about the right way to live seems to have a superior position. His statement seems to make sense. I want you to turn the tables on him and play his position.

Elaine. How do I do that?

Daniel. His proposition is: "The right way to A is to let everyone A the way they want to A." Substitute a B for his A. Any active verb.

Elaine. Well, let's see . . . worship?

Daniel. Try it and see.

Elaine. The right way to worship is to let everyone worship the way they want to worship.

Daniel. What do you think of it?

Elaine. It doesn't make any sense. Letting everyone worship the way they want to worship is not a way to worship.

Daniel. Try substituting a C.

Elaine [after a moment]. The right way to dance is to let everyone dance the way they want to dance. That doesn't make any sense, either.

Daniel. Why not?

Elaine. Because letting everyone dance the way they want to dance is not a way to dance.

Daniel. So what about the original statement?

Elaine. It tells you one thing you should do, but it doesn't tell you how to live. Letting everyone live the way they want to live is not a way to live.

Daniel. So it can hardly be the one *right* way to live.

Elaine. No.

Daniel [after some thought]. We haven't actually done anything new here. We always have to get behind people's words to see what's going on in their minds. In this case, what was going on was just some fuzzy thinking. Some fuzzy thinking that *sounded* good. We brought this to light by substituting different terms for his term, *live*. We have to be ready to try anything that will help us get behind the words to the ideas that generate the words.

Elaine. I don't seem to be much good at coming up with things to try.

Daniel. Well, I'll tell you something. When I started getting questions, back in 1992, each one of them initially flummoxed me. It was only after answering hundreds of them that the techniques I'm showing you became second nature to me. And even now I occasionally get one that stumps me. Not that I don't eventually crack it, but I have to go through the same steps we've been going through here, trying this and trying that until I see the answer.

Elaine. I guess I can take some consolation from that.

[They take a short break.]

Daniel. I'd like to get back to a subject we were discussing this morning. We were talking about tip-offs that set my alarms ringing, and I said you've got to keep an ear open for items that come to us from the received wisdom of our culture. For example, any statement that contains the word *Nature* is suspect — Nature in the sense of that *other* we see outside the window.

Elaine. How so?

Daniel. The received wisdom is that such a thing as Nature *exists*, that it is a veridical entity out there — as real and substantial as the US Congress or the Roman Catholic Church — enjoying a separate existence from our own. This is the entity people are thinking of when they say that they "love Nature" or would like to be "close to Nature."

Elaine. Well, there *is* a whole world of life out there that isn't human.

Daniel. And have we escaped from it?

Elaine. Escaped from it?

Daniel. People will often blame our problems on the fact that we have separated ourselves from Nature, that whole other world of life out there. Haven't you ever encountered this sentiment?

Elaine. Yes, I guess I have.

Daniel. So how far away from it are we?

Elaine. In reality, we're not far away from it at all.

Daniel. Then what sense does it make to say that it would be nice to be "close" to it? We can't *stop* being close to it. We're as much a part of that world as crickets or alligators or oak trees.

Elaine. You need some pretty thick blinders to miss that.

Daniel. The distinction between "us" and "it" is a cultural construct, and a very old one. It was clearly in place among the Hebrews, who certainly understood that humans belong to an order of being that is entirely separate from the rest of the living community. They knew that God didn't create the world for palm trees or jellyfish, he created it for humans. He doesn't concern himself with the doings of lizards or beetles. He concerns himself with the doings of humans. He didn't promise the dinosaurs a Messiah.

Elaine. True.

Daniel. And he didn't send his only-begotten son to save the wildlife and the rain forests.

Elaine. No.

Daniel. Considering your religious upbringing, I assume you're familiar with the Great Chain of Being concept.

Elaine. Yes.

Daniel. What's at the top of the chain?

Elaine. God.

Daniel. And below God?

Elaine. The angels.

Daniel. And below the angels?

Elaine. Humans.

Daniel. And below humans?

Elaine. Everything else.

Daniel. The Great Chain of Being concept is a product of the Middle Ages, but it wasn't left behind during the Renaissance. Descartes, Spinoza, and Leibniz all wrote about it with complete seriousness. In fact, it's never been left behind, has it? Even people who don't believe in God or angels still perceive Man to be at the top of the chain of life on this planet. He stands apart and above all the rest — the rest being that which during the Age of Enlightenment came to be known as "Nature."

Elaine. Yes.

Daniel. This is why I've always rejected "environmentalist" as a label for myself. In its fundamental vision, the environmentalist movement reinforces the idea that there is an "us" and an "it" — two separate things — when in fact what we have here is a single community.

Elaine. Yes, I see that. But even accepting all that, there will still be people who rank us as the most important members of that community.

Daniel. There's no doubt about that, and their reasons satisfy them. There are still people who rank the white race over all others, and their reasons satisfy them, too. There's really nothing to be said about this beyond pointing out that the community of life got along just fine without humans for billions of years. In terms of importance to the community as a whole, I would without hesitation rank earthworms above humans.

Elaine laughs.

Daniel. Well, let's see. Where to go next . . . Here's a question that should keep us occupied for a while: "Do you support the idea of extending human rights to primates?"

Elaine. I take it you don't.

Daniel. No, don't do that. You're not going to learn anything by leaping to what you assume to be my conclusion. Your job is to explore the assumptions of the person who asked this question. You have to understand his frame of reference and figure out why it seems like a sensible question to him.

Elaine. Okay. "Do you support the idea of extending human rights to primates?" It's loaded with assumptions.

Daniel. Let's hear them.

Elaine. I suppose the first one is the assumption that extending human rights to primates is something that's possible to do.

Daniel. Couldn't we do it with an act of Congress? Couldn't we persuade every government on the planet to do the same?

Elaine. Not as stated. Are we going to give primates — by the way, aren't *we* primates?

Daniel. Yes. Take the question as referring to nonhuman primates.

Elaine. Okay . . . Are we going to give them the right to vote, the right to bear arms?

Daniel. Ask the questioner. What would he say?

Elaine. He would say . . . let's see . . . "I mean the right to life, liberty, and the pursuit of happiness. The right to enjoy the protections of due process of law."

Daniel. So assuming that everyone in the world agreed to accord primates these rights, they'd be subject to eminent domain, the government's right to appropriate private property for public use. That's due process of law, isn't it?

Elaine. I guess so.

Daniel. And, under this assumption, if a gorilla killed a poacher, he wouldn't just be shot to death, he'd receive a fair trial.

Elaine. Well . . . he wouldn't be considered fit to participate in his own defense.

Daniel. True enough. So, in effect, all primates would have an irrevocable "Get out of jail free" card. Primates would have rights even humans don't have.

Elaine [after some thought]. I guess we'll have to settle for the right to life, liberty, and the pursuit of happiness.

Daniel. Okay. You said the question was loaded with assumptions. What are the others?

Elaine. Well . . . I guess one of them is the assumption that it makes sense to stop with primates. Is it because they're very intelligent? If you're going to extend human rights to intelligent creatures, then why not dolphins and elephants? Or if it's because they're endangered, then why not blue whales and bald eagles?

Daniel. So you're saying that the idea is unsupportable because of its arbitrary limitation of human rights to primates.

Elaine. No, not exactly. I guess I'm saying it's impractical, because no one is going to accept the extension of human rights to nonhuman primates as a stopping point. Maybe I shouldn't say no one. I mean that animal rights advocates aren't going to accept it. Why not minks and ermines, along with all the others I've mentioned? Vegetarians might want to extend human rights to chickens and cattle.

Daniel. True.

Elaine waits for Daniel to continue.

Daniel [after a minute or so]. You said the question was loaded with assumptions.

Elaine. Yes . . .

Daniel. You haven't touched on the most fundamental of these assumptions.

Elaine. Which one is that?

Daniel. Look for it.

Elaine. "Do you support the idea of extending human rights to primates?" Was that the question?

Daniel nods.

Elaine. I suppose there's an assumption that it's even *possible* to do such a thing. I mean, even with a worldwide agreement.

Daniel. Meaning what?

Elaine. Human rights are by definition *human*. How can you say that a lemur has *human* rights?

Daniel. It's a good point. But there's a much deeper one waiting to be found.

Elaine [after some thought]. I don't see what you're looking for.

Daniel. I'm not looking for it, *you* are . . . You're going to have to pull way, way back to see it.

Elaine thinks for a while, then shakes her head.

Daniel. Okay. I'm probably rushing things a bit here. What is meant by "human rights"? I'm not asking you to enumerate them. I'm asking you for a general definition: What are human rights?

Elaine. I guess I'd say that these are the rights people have by virtue of being human.

Daniel. In other words, to be human is to have these rights.

Elaine. That's right.

Daniel. Hold on a minute. [Brings Elaine a copy of *Key Ideas in Human Thought*, edited by Kenneth McLeish and published by Facts on File.] See how the term *human rights* is defined in this book.

Elaine [reading]. "Human rights are rights which all humans should possess because they are human beings irrespective of their citizenship, nationality, race, ethnicity, language, sex, sexuality, or abilities."

Daniel. Very similar to your own definition.

Elaine. Except for the word *should*. It says all humans *should* possess these rights, not that they do.

Daniel. What do you make of that?

Elaine. I'm not sure what to make of it.

Daniel. Suppose I were to define a college degree as a degree that all humans *should* possess. How would you react to that?

Elaine. I'd guess I'd ask, who says so?

Daniel. So does the author of this article ever explain who says that human rights are rights that all humans should possess simply because they're human beings?

Elaine [some minutes later, after reading the article]. The author describes it as a "doctrine," and the doctrine is a "lineal descendant of the doctrine of natural rights proposed by the founders of liberal political thought, notably John Locke."

Daniel. So the notion that there is such a thing as human rights is only about 350 years old.

Elaine. Yes. At least according to this source.

Daniel. I can run off a copy of the Hammurabi Code of Laws for you, but you can take my word for it that it contains no mention of "human rights." It lays out things that may and may not be done. One can say, though Hammurabi doesn't, that one has a right to do the things that he says may be done, but there's no implication that this right exists simply because one is human. This right exists because Hammurabi *says* it exists. He describes himself as "The king of righteousness, on whom Shamash has conferred right (or law)." "Or law" is in parentheses. I assume the translator is making the point that the word Hammurabi uses here can mean either *right* or *law*.

Elaine. What about the Bible? I assume you've checked that.

Daniel. Yes, of course. The word *right* appears many times, but most often in connection with the rights of the firstborn, which are just a matter of custom; in American society, for example, the firstborn has no special rights. There's nothing in the Bible like the concept of "human rights," rights that people have just because they're human. As with the Code of Hammurabi, the laws set down in the Bible can be seen as conferring rights — for example, the right to kill a witch — but these are exactly rights that are divinely *conferred*, not rights that are somehow innately human.

Elaine. Yes, that's true. Then there's the . . . I can't think of the name . . . the Magna Carta.

Daniel. Oh yes. This was a charter of rights granted by the English king to his barons in 1215.

Elaine. Certainly not *human* rights.

Daniel. No. Let me see that article on human rights . . . It says, "Unless human rights are specifically embodied in constitutional provisions, they are not legal rights." What do you suppose that means?

Elaine. I think it means . . . unless the country you're living in has a constitution that confers these rights on you, you don't really have them. You can't go to court and claim that your human rights have been violated unless the constitution says you have them.

Daniel. So, practically speaking, you don't have human rights just by being human after all. If you have them, it's because the constitution says you have them.

Elaine. I'd say so. But doesn't the US Constitution say that these rights are God-given?

Daniel. No. You're thinking of the Declaration of Independence, though it doesn't use that particular expression. It says that all men are "endowed by their Creator with certain unalienable Rights," among which are life, liberty, and the pursuit of happiness.

Elaine. Unalienable being what?

Daniel. Unalienable being "incapable of being taken away from or given away by the possessor." It's a curious word. Its sole application seems to be to rights. Its first such application was made in 1611.

Elaine. Okay. But this is just an assertion, isn't it? That all men are endowed by their Creator with certain unalienable Rights.

Daniel. Certainly. I have a quote about this. Hold on a second . . . Here's what Thomas Jefferson,* the principal author, wrote in support of what's said in the declaration: "Neither aiming at originality of principle or sentiment, nor yet copied from any particular and previous writing, it was intended to be an expression of the American mind, and to give to that expression the proper tone and spirit called for by the occasion. All its authority rests then on the harmonizing sentiments of the day,

---

*President Kennedy repeated the assertion in his inaugural address, saying, "The rights of man come not from the generosity of the state, but from the hand of God."

whether expressed in conversation, in letters, printed essays, or in the elementary books of public right, as Aristotle, Cicero, Locke, Sidney, et cetera." Of course he wasn't referring specifically to the expression we're considering.

Elaine. Wasn't he a Deist?

Daniel. Jefferson's religious beliefs are the subject of endless debate. He certainly never specifically claimed to be a Deist, though there's little doubt that he was influenced by and sympathetic with Deistic views. His reference in the declaration to "Nature's God" certainly has a Deistic flavor. Why do you ask?

Elaine. I'm looking for his grounds for saying that the Creator endowed us with inalienable rights. They weren't scriptural.

Daniel. No. "Nature's God" isn't the God of the Bible. He — or it — is the "uncaused cause" of the cosmological argument. Roughly speaking, it goes like this: "Since the universe exists, it must have had a cause, and since a causal chain can't stretch infinitely backward in time, there must be a first cause that was not itself caused; this uncaused first cause is God." This argument speaks only to the existence of God and posits nothing about his character.

Elaine. But it was this God who endowed us with inalienable rights. It's still just an assertion.

Daniel. Rights can *only* be asserted or denied. In the end, they're just something to be argued about. One side asserts the right and the other side denies it, but there's no final authority — final in the sense that it's an authority accepted by both sides — that can be appealed to in order to end the argument. Even the law can't be appealed to, because almost any law can be changed if enough people want it changed.

Elaine [after some thought]. But the argument over slavery was eventually settled, wasn't it? I mean, even in the South, I doubt if you could find many slavery advocates nowadays.

Daniel. Arguments aren't necessarily settled just because no one is around to make them. There's no one around today — at least in the United States — to make the arguments that were put forward in support of slavery as a moral option in the 1860s, but the arguments are still there. The Pelagian argument is still there, even though the church finally pronounced against it. The argument over abortion has been won in the United States, but it obviously hasn't been settled.

Elaine. Yes, I see your point.

Daniel. By contrast, the argument over the famous cold-fusion results of the late 1980s* was eventually settled, because both sides of the argument accept the scientific method as a final authority. The results of that particular experiment couldn't be reproduced, and that was that.

Elaine [after some thought]. I'm feeling a bit lost. Where are we here?

Daniel. We're still looking at assumptions in the question "Do you support the idea of extending human rights to primates?" What have we concluded so far?

Elaine. I'd say that we've concluded that "human rights" is another cultural construct.

Daniel. By implication, the author of the article in *Key Ideas in Human Thought* seems to agree with us, since he says that these are rights that people *should* have, not that they *do* have.

---

*Allegedly produced by chemists Stanley Pons of the University of Utah and Martin Fleischmann of the University of Southampton.

Elaine. He also indicates that it's not at all universally agreed that such things exist.

Daniel. While you're at it, look up the entry on *rights*.

Elaine [after finding her place in the book]. There isn't one.

Daniel. Odd, isn't it? The concept of rights seems even more fundamental than the concept of human rights, and has a longer history. What is a right, anyway?

Elaine. I'd say it's an entitlement. An entitlement to have or do something.

Daniel. I've searched many dictionaries of aboriginal languages, and very few of them seem to have a word for *right* in this sense. In all the reading I've done about aboriginal peoples, I've never come across any instance of them arguing about rights or asserting a right to do the things they do.

Elaine. It would surprise me if you had. But that's just an intuitive reaction.

Daniel. Why do *we* have to assert rights to do the things we want to do?

Elaine. That's an interesting question.

Daniel. A hundred years ago homosexual acts were almost universally outlawed in the West, France and Poland being two exceptions I know of. The situation is entirely different today.

Elaine. And you're going to ask why.

Daniel. Of course.

Elaine. It's different because homosexuals asserted their right to have sex with people of the same gender and eventually gained enough support to win it.

Daniel. Obviously. A whole lot of people think they have the right to decide what people can and can't do in their bedrooms. This was the only tool they had to use against them. The asserting of rights has become an important tool for the people of our culture, but my point is . . . ?

Elaine. That it's only the people of our culture who need to use it.

Daniel. To us, having to assert a right in order to have the things we want or want to do is taken to be a sort of human norm. It seems to make perfect sense — to be not in the least bizarre. One of my tasks has been to pull people far enough away from our culture to see how very bizarre it really is. I don't mean that it's uniquely bizarre. I just mean that, seen from a distance — from the point of view of a Martian anthropologist — our culture is no less bizarre than cultures whose customs seem to us outlandishly grotesque. Our way of doing things would seem as bizarre to the Gebusi of New Guinea as the Gebusi's way of doing things seems to us.

Daniel [after a half-hour break]. In *Beyond Civilization* and elsewhere I presented an important observation made by Buckminster Fuller: "You never change things by fighting the existing reality. To change something, build a new model that makes the existing model obsolete."

Elaine. Yes, I remember.

Daniel. This is a "hard saying," and I'm glad to have Bucky Fuller to blame for it.

Elaine [after some thought]. People have a lot of faith in the utility of fighting the existing reality.

Daniel. For most people, or at least a great many people, fighting is all they can see to do — or, practically speaking, all they *can* do — even if it doesn't "change things." I had this question from a reader: "Do we never resort to battle? I mean, if the last two ibex are standing in the last unplowed field and are about to be shot, and all attempts at mind change have failed, what do we do?" How would you answer this?

Elaine. Well . . . battle? I'd have to say yes.

Daniel. Who do you suppose is about to shoot these last two ibex?

Elaine. I don't know. Poachers, I'd assume.

Daniel. So you drive off these poachers or kill them outright. The problem's solved.

Elaine. No . . . The poachers can always come back, or other poachers can come.

Daniel. So?

Elaine. So you'd have to post an armed guard. Five or ten men.

Daniel. For how long?

Elaine. I don't know . . . Until the ibex multiplied.

Daniel. Then you could withdraw the armed guards.

Elaine shakes her head.

Daniel. No? What then?

Elaine. If poachers — or hunters or whoever — killed off all but two ibex in the first place, there's nothing stopping them from doing the same thing again.

Daniel. So you'd need to maintain the guards, even increase their number, since they'd have more ibex to protect. For how long?

Elaine [sighing]. Indefinitely. Forever.

Daniel lets her think about it.

Elaine. Fighting the existing reality certainly doesn't change things in this case.

Daniel. In all my writings I stress the fact that if people go on thinking the way they generally do now, we're doomed. Nothing can save us but changing the minds of the people around us. Lots of readers don't like to hear this, because they want *action*, and this doesn't seem like action to them.

Elaine. Battling the poachers is *action*.

Daniel. Yes, exactly. The fact is, however, that if most of the people who live around those two ibex don't care whether they live or die, then those ibex are doomed. But if the people who live around those ibex see the world in a different way, then it's the *poachers* who are doomed. There's just no shortcut. The present existing reality is that people in general fail to see that systematically attacking the diversity of the living community is going to be fatal to *us*. Until that changes, no amount of fighting is going to save us.

Elaine. That makes our situation look hopeless.

Daniel. Not at all. The intellectual climate has changed dramatically in the past fifteen years. The number of mind-changing books that are being published climbs every year. What we're looking for is what Malcolm Gladwell called the "tipping point," the point where an accumulation of very small things — often quite suddenly and unexpectedly — produces an enormous change. The collapse of the Soviet Union is an excellent example. No intelligence service in the world predicted it or had the slightest clue that it was about to happen. The chance that significant change could occur there also "looked hopeless" — until it suddenly happened.

Elaine. What things do you think contributed to that tipping point?

Daniel [laughing]. A few years ago, in some speech or other, I suggested (not very forcefully) that rock music played an important role in it. I would never have dared to put such an outrageous idea in print until Andras Simonyi, Hungary's ambassador to the United States, said the same thing, very forthrightly, last year. He spent an hour talking about it at the Rock and Roll Hall of Fame. I remember that Western music was described as "an open window of fresh air in a very repressive society." That window stayed open for decades and clearly affected the way young people saw their world.

Elaine. I was wondering . . . Someplace you once said that politicians would be the last to "get it." Why is that?

Daniel. You can figure that out.

Elaine. Oh. Yeah. Sometimes I wonder why I've got a head.

Daniel. Don't be too hard on yourself. I've been asked the same question by other people who couldn't figure it out either.

Elaine. We're used to thinking of politicians as leaders. Or that they're *supposed* to be leaders, want to be *perceived* as leaders.

Daniel. Uh-huh.

Elaine. Whatever you may think about it, George Bush certainly did lead us — or mislead us — into the war against Iraq.

Daniel. No argument there.

Elaine. What am I missing here?

Daniel. What do I keep telling you to do when you get stuck?

Elaine. Pull back. Look at it from a higher angle.

Daniel offers no help.

Elaine. Okay . . . I've been fixating on their role or supposed role, once elected. I need to look at how they *get* elected . . . Or rather, *who* elects them. The public is not going to elect a president who says . . . "Look, we can't just think about the next four years. We've got to think about the whole human future — that's what's at risk."

Daniel. Why couldn't such a candidate get elected?

Elaine. Because the segment of the public that would vote for him is too small at this point.

Daniel. Go on. You still haven't explained why I say that politicians will be the last to get it.

Elaine. They won't get it till they *have* to get it. In other words, they won't have to change until the electorate changes. When a majority of the electorate gets it, then only the candidates who get it will get elected.

Daniel. Good. Now see if you can wrap it up.

Elaine. Wrap it up?

Daniel. In a neat little package.

Elaine [*after some thought*]. Politicians don't educate the electorate. The electorate educates politicians, with their votes.

Daniel. For good or ill.

Elaine. Yes.

Daniel. Excellent.

Saturday: Morning

Daniel. Here's a tricky little question that came in recently: "What biological mechanisms would allow us to keep our population at a level compatible with our food supply?"

Elaine. What does he mean by "biological mechanisms"?

Daniel. I doubt if he knows himself. I think what he means are mechanisms that are not political — for example, government limitations on food production that are not legalistic, like limiting family size by law, and that don't depend on self-restraint, like birth control.

Elaine. That still doesn't tell me what a biological mechanism is.

Daniel [after some consideration]. I'm beginning to see this as a tendency of yours: to pick out one element of a question and fixate on it. You're not thinking about the question as a whole.

Elaine. I guess you're right. How does it go again?

Daniel repeats the question.

Elaine. Okay . . . Well, I can see one assumption he's making: that there *are* biological mechanisms that would allow us to keep our population at a level compatible with our food supply.

Daniel. Uh-huh.

Elaine [after a long silence]. What else can I say? You've never said there are biological mechanisms that would allow humans to keep their populations at levels compatible with our food supply, have you?

Daniel. No, I've never said anything like that.

Elaine. So he's making an unwarranted assumption and asking you to verify it.

Daniel [sighing]. Elaine, this person is fundamentally confused, and you've bought into his confusion. In effect, you're saying, "Okay, I'll accept without question that what you're saying makes sense." He didn't really *look* at what he was saying, and if *you* don't really look at it, then you're no better off than he is. You did the same thing with the person who suggested that the one right way for people to live is to let everyone live the way they want to live. You've got to stop meeting every challenge with acquiescence.

Elaine. Well, this is discouraging.

Daniel. You shouldn't think of it that way at all. I have to assume that the person who wrote the question, being a reader of serious books, is of above-average intelligence, and the question itself isn't a dumb one, despite its fundamental confusion. And . . . you know it's my intention to publish a transcript of this conversation we're having.

Elaine. Yes . . . ?

Daniel. I'll wager that, at this point, among the readers who are following the discussion of this particular question, 99.99 percent of them will be just as stumped as you are.

Elaine laughs. I suppose that's reassuring.

Daniel. The answers I give to people's questions — and the conclusions I reach in general — seem to astonish my readers, seem to be unexpected . . . alien. And the whole purpose of what we're doing here is to shed some light on how I produce these answers and conclusions. The process seems unexceptional to me, but it obviously doesn't seem so to my readers — or to you.

Elaine. That's certainly true.

Daniel. All right. So let's return to the basics. What are this questioner's assumptions?

Elaine. Well, let's see. First, there's the assumption that there are "biological mechanisms" that will achieve what he wants to achieve.

Daniel. We've already looked at that one.

Elaine. Okay. Then there's his assumption that . . . I'm trying to remember how he put it . . . It's his assumption that we need to keep our population at a level compatible with our food supply.

Daniel. Yes, that is one of his assumptions.

Elaine [after some thought]. I'm stuck. I don't see any others.

Daniel. It isn't stated directly. It's implicit in his question. That's why you have to look behind the words.

Elaine spends a couple of minutes on it, then shakes her head.

Daniel. I'd rather not ask you leading questions, but it looks like I'll have to. What is his concern, his worry?

Elaine. That our population is not at a level that is compatible with our food supply.

Daniel. Yes, this is implicit in his question.

Elaine [doubtfully]. Okay.

Daniel. Well, *look* at it.

Elaine [after a minute]. Are you saying that our population —

Daniel. No, don't do that. Don't go fishing for the answer in my head. Work it out yourself.

Elaine. But the only alternative I can see is that our population *is* compatible with our food supply.

Daniel waits.

Elaine. Okay, I've got it. Or I think I do.

Daniel. Which is it?

Elaine. I've got it.

Daniel. Go ahead.

Elaine. Our population *is* compatible with our food supply. At all times. When there was food for three billion of us, there were three billion of us. When there was food for six billion of us, there were six billion of us. If there hadn't been food for six billion, there wouldn't *be* six billion.

Daniel. So what "biological mechanism" makes population "compatible with food supply"?

Elaine. I don't know what to call it. Supply and maintenance? The population of every species grows to a point that is "compatible" with the food available to it. When food availability increases, its population increases. When food availability decreases, its population decreases . . . But not everyone agrees that this is the way it works, do they?

Daniel. For nonhuman species, there's no disagreement at all. But many people — including even many biologists — still cling to the doctrine of human exceptionalism, the way many Christian fundamentalists still cling to the doctrine of creationism.

Elaine. I don't think I've heard of that — human exceptionalism.

Daniel. In this context, it's just the doctrine that, among all the hundreds of millions of species in the living community, the human species is the sole exception to the rule you just described: that population increases or decreases according to food availability.

Elaine. How do they explain that? I mean, what are their grounds for accepting this idea?

Daniel. I've never seen a defense of it, but I imagine it stems from the fact that, as individuals, we can choose to reproduce or not. The fact that — as a species — our growth began to soar as soon as we began to increase food availability at will seems to them a mere coincidence. The record of the past ten thousand years, after some three million years of relative population stability, holds no significance for them.* In effect, they deny that the Agricultural Revolution had anything to do with our growth from a few hundred million to six billion.

Elaine. That hardly seems rational.

Daniel. Almost nothing exerts a more powerful hold on people's minds than unexamined and unchallenged received wisdom — and human exceptionalism is certainly a part of that legacy. In fact, it must have seemed quite daring back in 2001 when a peer-reviewed scientific journal actually published a paper

---

*Peter Farb, a distinguished naturalist, linguist, and anthropologist, perceived it as a paradox: "Intensification of production to feed an increased population leads to a still greater increase in population."

affirming the connection between population and food availability.*

Elaine. It's amazing to me that that should seem daring.

Daniel. Trust me, the doctrine of human exceptionalism is deep set in Mother Culture's heart . . . Here's a little story you'll find amusing that isn't entirely off the point. *[Goes to get a book.]* In the very early stages of work on the book that ultimately became *Ishmael,* I wanted to know if there was any estimate of the human population before the Agricultural Revolution. As I later learned, there are many different estimates, but I first turned to a reference I had on hand, the *Dunlop Illustrated Encyclopedia of Facts,* published in 1969. Unlike like most books of its kind, which are either assembled by nameless staff workers or are collections of articles by various authorities, this one had a single pair of authors, Norris and Ross McWhirter, who were clearly not averse to expressing conclusions as well as facts. They didn't have the particular information I was looking for, but in an article on "Growth of the Human Population" I found a very useful chart of population estimates for roughly the past two thousand years and extending thirty years ahead to the year 2000, where they correctly estimated it would be around six billion. Following the chart was this observation: "If this trend continues, the world has only fifteen generations left before the human race breeds itself to an overcrowded extinction. By 2600 AD there would be one person per square yard of habitable land surface." It's their next statement that was of special importance: "Increasing food production merely aggravates the problem by broadening the base of the expansion and hastening rather than postponing the end." And I thought, "Well, of course. That's obvious."

---

*"Human Population Numbers as a Function of Food Supply" by Russell Hopfenberg and David Pimentel, *Environment, Development and Sustainability* 3 (2001): 1–15.

Elaine. It *is* obvious.

Daniel. And because it seemed so obvious, my original presentation in *Ishmael* of the connection between food production and population growth was almost offhand. I soon found out that what is obvious to you and me is very far from being obvious to the public at large. I expanded my presentation of the subject for the paperback edition, but from the public's reaction I could see that this was still not enough. In *The Story of B* I presented the subject at even greater length — and it still wasn't enough. One night at some personal appearance (I don't recall where it was) the subject of food production and population growth came up again, and after some discussion one audience member stood up and stormed out after declaring that I was the most obscene person she'd ever encountered.

Elaine. I can't understand that.

Daniel. Ah, but you see, despite the fact that "Increasing food production merely aggravates the problem by broadening the base of the expansion," we *must* increase food production.

Elaine. Why?

Daniel. You know the answer to that.

Elaine. To feed the starving millions.

Daniel. Of course. You see, the assertion had been made that I couldn't just "let the starving millions starve." My reply was that I'm not God. I don't "let" earthquakes happen, I don't "let" plagues occur, I don't "let" hurricanes and tornadoes happen — and I don't "let" people starve. This reply is what made me an obscenity.

Elaine. Yes, I see. But — forgive me — we don't have any *choice* in the matter of hurricanes and tornadoes and earthquakes.

Daniel. First, I don't want to hear any more of that "forgive me" stuff. I don't want your acquiescence. I don't want you to accept things just because they come out of my mouth.

Elaine. Okay. I'm sorry. I didn't even hear myself saying it.

Daniel. Okay. We can't as yet do anything about hurricanes and tornadoes and earthquakes, but we *can* do something about hunger. The example I hear about most often is the starving millions in Africa. We *can* ship enough food over there to feed them all. So? Take it from there.

Elaine looks at him blankly.

Daniel. You're not here to listen to my answers. You're here to find them for yourself.

Elaine. God . . . I don't know where to begin.

Daniel. All right, I'll get you started. Why are they starving?

Elaine. Well, obviously because they don't have enough food.

Daniel. Come on, Elaine. That's just the definition of starving. Why don't they have enough food?

Elaine. Because . . . because the population has outstripped local resources.

Daniel. And why has this happened?

Elaine. Well, either their local resources have diminished or their population has grown beyond the point where it can be supported by local resources.

Daniel. Or both. As any population grows, its food supply diminishes. This is perfectly predictable. It's a cycle familiar to any biologist. As a population grows, it depletes its food supply. And as its food supply diminishes, the population begins to decline.

As the population declines, its food supply begins to recover. As its food supply recovers, the population grows. As the population grows, its food supply begins to diminish. And so on. This is the way it works throughout the living community: populations growing and declining as food availability grows and declines.

Elaine. I see that.

Daniel. Then why are so many millions of Africans starving?

Elaine. Because they've outstripped the food that's available to them locally.

Daniel. So their population is declining.

Elaine. No, because we've said, "We're not going to *let* their population decline."

Daniel. They're starving, but, thanks to our generosity, they're staying alive. And because they're staying alive . . . ?

Elaine. They can reproduce and bring up a new generation to starve.

Daniel. Which we can generously keep alive so that they can reproduce and bring up yet another generation to starve. Our benevolence is breathtaking.

Elaine. If we left them alone, their population would decline to the point where they could live within their own resources.

Daniel. But it would be immoral to let that happen. Better that more of them should starve on our beneficence than fewer live tolerably within their own food resources.

Elaine. Yes, apparently.

Daniel. How did it come about that their populations grew to a point where they could no longer live within their own local food resources?

Elaine. I hadn't thought about that . . . We've put a lot of effort into helping them build up their populations. Eliminating disease, lowering infant mortality. Showing them how to increase food production. Helping them convert their lands to cash crops for export.

Daniel. For hundreds of thousands of years they'd been living perfectly well where they were and as they were, but they weren't living *up to our standards*, and it's our divine mandate that everyone in the world must be made to live the way we live, whatever the cost. It would have been *immoral* for us to leave them alone, just as it would be immoral for us to leave them alone now. Much better to send them food to maintain them in a state of perpetual starvation than to let their populations decline to a point where they can live within their own resources.

Elaine. I suspect that would be the typical reaction.

Daniel. What would God do, if we stopped feeding them?

Elaine. God?

Daniel. God wouldn't let them starve, would he?

Elaine. Based on past performance, I think he would. He hasn't intervened in human affairs in a long, long time.

Daniel. God would let them starve, but we have to be better than God. We *are* better than God, which is why it's so appropriate that we should rule the world.

Elaine. Yes. I can see why this woman thought you were the most obscene person she'd ever met.

Daniel laughs. We Martians are fiends . . . Let's move on. I hope we're finished with these issues for good.

Elaine. There's one more I have to bring up, because people keep bringing it up to *me*.

Daniel. Okay.

Elaine. It goes something like this. If population is a function of food availability, then why is it that the developed nations, in which food is plentiful, have the lowest growth rate — and sometimes a zero or negative growth rate — while undeveloped nations, in which food is scarce, have higher growth rates?

Daniel [sighing]. Yes, of course, there's that one. This represents a kind of misdirection called "changing the subject." Have I said anything connecting growth rate to food availability?

Elaine [after thinking for a moment]. Not that I recall.

Daniel. I've said only that the population of any species will grow if more food becomes available to it, and our population is currently growing by about seventy-seven million every year. That may not sound like much, but I once took the trouble to do some research, and found that this is equivalent to the combined populations of Canada, Australia, Denmark, Austria, and Greece. Every year.

Elaine. That's impressive, when you put it that way.

Daniel. The fact that it's growing at a faster rate in some places than others is beside the point. The point is that the human population is steadily growing because we're steadily increasing food production.

Elaine. I see that.

Daniel. The reason why growth rates differ in developed and undeveloped nations has nothing to do with food availability. It has to do with family economics. In developed nations having a multiplicity of children is a burden, no matter how abundant food is, whereas in undeveloped nations it's a blessing, no matter how scarce food is. Do I need to explain why this is so?

Elaine. No, I don't think so. In developed nations it costs a lot of money to raise children, and they're not expected to contribute anything to family income. In undeveloped nations it costs little to raise children, and they generally contribute a lot to family income.

Daniel. I'm sure you realize that we don't consume all the food we produce in the United States.

Elaine. Of course. I assume we export huge amounts of it.

Daniel. So this food isn't being turned into human biomass in the United States. Since it's not here, it *can't* be used for that purpose.

Elaine. Right.

Daniel. So what's happening to it?

Elaine. It's being turned into human biomass in other parts of the world.

Daniel. So while we're not interested in increasing our own population, we're very interested in producing surplus food to support population growth elsewhere.

Elaine. True. *[After thinking for a bit.]* But when this business of growth rates is brought up, one of the points that people make is that when currently underdeveloped nations reach our level of prosperity their growth rates are likely to go down just the way ours has.

Daniel. And at that point population growth will be negligible.

Elaine. That's right.

Daniel. All right. We need a reality check here. First, it's been estimated that we'd need the resources of six planets the size of the earth if all six billion of us were living the way people live in developed nations. Second, the US Census Bureau estimates that by the year 2050, there will be nine billion of us, and while the growth rate will have declined substantially, we'll still be adding an annual population the size of New York City and Los Angeles combined. Third, you understand that our present system of food production is almost entirely dependent on fossil fuel at every stage between fertilization of cropland to delivery of processed, packaged foods to your grocery store.

Elaine. Yes.

Daniel. Fourth, the projected increase in our population to nine billion assumes that food production is going to increase. But this projection doesn't take into account the fact that, in order to reach nine billion, we're going to have to steadily increase the amount of fossil fuel we pour into agricultural production during a fifty-year period when the world's supply of fossil fuel is going to be steadily diminishing. It's estimated that oil production is going to decline by 60 or 70 percent between now and the year 2050.

Elaine. So it sounds like that projection is based on a fantasy.

Daniel. Yes. If our system of agriculture and the percentage of oil used for agriculture remain the same for the next fifty years, then our population is also going to decline by 60 or 70 percent.

Elaine. The die-off predicted by the Peak Oil theory.

Daniel. That's right. At a conference this year in Dublin* a paper was read that examined what we'd need to do to restructure our agricultural system to one that is fossil-fuel-free and concluded that this was not beyond possibility.† So the threatened die-off is not necessarily inevitable, at least during this period. I seriously doubt that the planet's ecological systems could survive a human population of nine billion — nine billion and still growing.

Elaine [after thinking for a minute]. So — in light of all this — the difference in growth rates between developed and undeveloped nations really seems like a nonissue.

Daniel. It's a red herring. Thrown out to distract from the fact that, like all other species, our overall population grows when our food supply grows, no matter whether growth occurs faster in one place or another . . . Well, let's see . . . *[Picks up and begins looking through a stack of index cards]*

Elaine. I have a question.

Daniel. Go ahead.

Elaine. Is it the plan that we're going to continue with questions you've received from readers?

---

*"What Will We Eat as the Oil Runs Out?" organized by the Foundation for the Economics of Sustainability (FEASTA), 2005.
†"Threats of Peak Oil to the Global Food Supply" by Richard Heinberg, author of two important books in the Peak Oil canon, *The Party's Over* and *Powerdown*.

Daniel. Well . . . I hadn't so much thought of it as a plan as . . . Do you have a problem with it as a procedure?

Elaine. Not a problem, exactly.

Daniel. But?

Elaine. I guess I expected something more . . . systematic.

Daniel. Talk some more.

Elaine. You're teaching me how to deal with questions. But in reality — in my day-to-day life — I don't have to deal with questions. No one has ever asked me questions like the ones we've been discussing.

Daniel. I'm not teaching you how to answer questions. Have we ever actually answered any of the questions I've brought up?

Elaine. Well, no, not specifically. I mean, we've never ended up framing an actual answer.

Daniel. The questions are just raw material. They give us opportunities to examine what's going on in the minds of the people around us.

Elaine. I don't know . . .

Daniel. Consider this. Once I was listening to a talk show in the car, and the subject under discussion was the protection of endangered species. The host said something like, "I don't know. Personally, I can do without songbirds."

Elaine. Uh-huh.

Daniel. You see that I could have used this as a springboard for an examination of what was going on in this person's mind.

Elaine. Yes, certainly.

Daniel. But it's not a question that someone sent to me. It's something I picked out of the air.

Elaine. I get that.

Daniel. My point is that I don't have a stock of material to look at that I've heard on the radio. What I have is a stock of questions and comments that people have sent to me.

Elaine. I see that . . .

Daniel. But?

Elaine. I don't know.

Daniel. Take your time. Take all the time you need.

Elaine [after a few minutes]. Right at the beginning, you talked about one big question that you felt you'd never answered adequately. And the idea seemed to be that you were going to answer it here, in this conversation.

Daniel. The question being "How do I do what I do?"

Elaine. That's right.

Daniel. And you feel we're not getting at that question.

Elaine. Maybe it would be more accurate to say that *I'm* not getting at it. At least that's the way I feel.

Daniel. Well, if that's the way you *feel*, then that's the way it *is*. Tell me more about it.

Elaine. I guess what I'm looking for is your *method*. A coherent, systematic description of your method.

Daniel. You're looking for something like that classic by Charles Van Doren and Mortimer Adler, *How to Read a Book*. That was very methodical, very coherent and systematic.

Elaine. I haven't read it, but I'll take your word for it.

Daniel [after a few minutes]. Back in the mid-1970s I had a wonderful tennis instructor. I hadn't played tennis in twenty years, and I'd never had any formal instruction at all. So the first thing he did, once we had me properly outfitted, was to put me on a court, stand three or four yards away, and bounce a ball to my forehand to see what I did with it. Then after a while he started bouncing balls to my backhand. Then he said, "Okay, we've got to work on your basic strokes." So he taught me the proper way to step into a ball coming to my right or left. I practiced these strokes — oh, I don't know — five thousand times, so many times that I could stand up right now and without hesitation show you exactly how the ball was addressed in the era when Jimmy Connors and John McEnroe were superstars of tennis. When we had these strokes down, we added volleys at the net, then smashes, then serves. During this long, long period we never "played tennis," never just rallied, never played games and kept score. I don't suppose you see why I'm telling you this.

Elaine. You're right, I don't.

Daniel. I can't teach you that way. Call it the *technical* way, in which you perfect all the individual techniques and only then begin to put them all together.

Elaine. Okay. I guess I can see that.

Daniel. I suppose you could say that the technical way is opposite from the way you learn to ride a bicycle. You can't learn to ride a bicycle first by practicing steering for fifty hours, pedaling for fifty hours, and keeping your balance for fifty hours. You get all those skills at once, in one instant, or you never get them at all. One minute you're just falling down a lot and the next you're riding a bicycle.

Elaine. That's true.

Daniel. But it may be useful to you — or give you a feeling of coherence and system — if we review the various skills that are involved in doing what I do.

Elaine. I think so, yes.

Daniel. I guess the first of these is simply alertness to nonsense. When that talk-show host said he could get along perfectly well without songbirds, a million people heard him and thought nothing of it. I picked up on it instantly and recognized it as the blather of an empty-headed fool.

Elaine. I think I would've, too.

Daniel. Ten years ago? That's about when I heard it.

Elaine [after thinking about it]. Honestly, probably not. I probably would've thought, "Well, that's true. I'd miss them, but I could live without them."

Daniel. Okay. So you're more alert now than you were then. But you can see that there's no way to give you lessons in alertness. I mean, I can't say, "Now we're going to spend the next ten hours working on your alertness to nonsense."

Elaine. No, I don't see how you could do that.

Daniel. So what's the second step in the "Quinn method"?

Elaine. You try to understand the thinking that produced the nonsense. You look for the assumption or assumptions behind it.

Daniel. And what's the assumption in this case?

Elaine [after a moment's thought]. That the reason birds are here — their function in the workings of the world — is to provide humans with entertainment.

Daniel. And what's the third step?

Elaine. I guess I'd say it's . . . extending this assumption . . . connecting it to more general assumptions.

Daniel. In this case?

Elaine. The assumption that the world and everything in it was made specifically for Man's benefit.

Daniel. Do you see a fourth step?

Elaine [after some thought]. No, I can't say that I do.

Daniel. Having found the more general assumption behind this particular notion, you look at some of the other notions or actions this assumption gives rise to. For example?

Elaine. I'd say . . . working from this assumption, we're free to eliminate any species that inconveniences us. Wolves, coyotes, and so on. If they're valueless to us, then they're superfluous. They don't do anything for us, so they don't need to be here, and we can get rid of them . . . And in general we can do anything we want to the world. It's our toy — God gave it to us — and we can do anything we like with it, including smashing it to bits.

Daniel. Very good.

Elaine. But I'd still like to see . . . "How you do what you do" isn't just limited to little things like this. I'd like to see how doing what you do produces your books.

Daniel. Well, you remember that I did start with the bit of nonsense that got me started, the idea that a nuclear holocaust would throw us back to the Stone Age.

Elaine. And what about *Ishmael?*

Daniel. I talked about that some. The received wisdom that the true story of Man begins with the Agricultural Revolution — that the first three million years didn't amount to anything worth talking about.

Elaine. And what *did* they amount to?

Daniel. You mean in terms of opera houses built and flying machines invented? Symphonies composed? The laws of physics described? Nothing, of course.

Elaine. What then?

Daniel. You don't think you can answer this?

Elaine. I wish I could. Don't you think I've thought about it?

Daniel. And came up with nothing?

Elaine. Nothing but trivial things like fire, the bow and arrow, and maybe the wheel.

Daniel. You know these things are trivial?

Elaine. Of course.

Daniel. Well, that's something. What humanity came up with and held on to during its first three million years was a social organization that worked well for *people.* It didn't work well for *products,* for motorboats and can openers and operettas. It didn't work well for the greedy, the ruthless, and the power hungry. That's what *we* have, a social organization that works beautifully for products — which just keep getting better and better every year — but very poorly for people, except for the greedy, the ruthless, and the power hungry. Our ancestors lived in societies that every anthropologist agrees were nonhierarchical and markedly egalitarian. They weren't structured so that a few at the top lived lives of luxury, a few more lived in the middle in comfort, and the masses at the bottom lived in poverty or near poverty, just struggling to survive. They weren't riddled with crime, depression, madness, suicide, and addiction. And when we came along with invitations to join our glorious civilization, they fought to the death to hold on to the life they had. You knew that.

Elaine. Yes.

Daniel. Back in the 1990s I kept track of South American tribes whose members were committing suicide in preference to being sucked into our orbit. Hold on a second. *[Goes to his computer, brings up a file, and reads from it.]* Just a few examples . . . July 1993: "The Yanomami, an ancient Amazon tribal people, are committing suicide. . . . The rape of their land, in the rain forests of Roraima in northern Brazil, by thousands of *garimpeiros* (wildcat gold and tin miners) and the diseases they bring that are killing the Yanomami in frightening numbers, are too much for these primitive people to bear. What pressure groups refer to as a genocide has led three young Yanomami to kill themselves in the past six weeks, a phenomenon alien to their culture, which forbids even talk of death." May 1997, Brazil: "Anthropologists say the Guarani-Kaiowa already have lost more than half their ancestral lands to ranchers. Rather than give up their traditional lifestyle, at least 235 of the Indians have taken their lives in recent years, according to official records." June 1997: "In Colombia, the U'wa tribe . . . has threat-

ened mass suicide if Oxy" — the Occidental Petroleum
Corporation — "encroaches on its territory." December 1997:
"Every 15 days, a Guarani-Kaiowa Indian commits suicide, a
Brazilian Indian rights group says. In 1997, 27 members of the
Brazilian tribe committed suicide, bringing the total to 158 in
the past 11 years."

Elaine. Uh-huh. Of course most people probably just think
they're foolish — don't realize what they're missing.

Daniel. Just as most people don't realize what these peoples
have — don't realize why they'd rather die than give it up . . . In
any case, what humanity came up with during these first three
million years was a way of life that works well *for people* and
that is *sustainable* — that could have promised life for
humankind for millions of years more — an accomplishment
greater than any of ours, though of course less flashy.

Elaine. But you're not suggesting that "coming up with it" was a
conscious achievement. I mean, nobody *invented* the tribal life.

Daniel. Of course not. It was nonetheless the outgrowth of
human intelligence and experience. What *didn't* work (and
one has to suppose that things were tried that didn't work) was
abandoned — and abandoned by people who *knew* it wasn't
working. What was left after all the trials was the tribe, which
was *evolutionarily stable,* meaning not that it was perfect but
that hundreds of thousands of years of natural selection — on
a social level — was unable to produce an organization that
worked better. To my mind the evolution of the tribe was an
accomplishment of greater importance to the human race than
all the advances of the Industrial Revolution put together. If we
were still living tribally, we'd be facing a future measured in
millions of years. As it is, we've walked on the moon but are

now facing a future that can be measured in decades, if we go on living the way we're presently living.

Elaine. Well, I can certainly see that . . . While I think of it, a friend once asked me how I know that people ten thousand years ago were living the way present-day aboriginal peoples live.

Daniel. That's interesting. A friend of *mine* asked the very same question. He is, or was, a historian.

Elaine. How did you answer him?

Daniel. What's the thinking behind the question, coming as it did from a historian?

Elaine. I would say he was thinking . . . people in historical times have constantly changed their style of living. I mean the organizational systems under which they live.

Daniel. Give me some examples.

Elaine. Oh, it's been too long . . . After the fall of the Roman Empire, there was feudalism. After feudalism . . .

Daniel. The secular, centralized state. Mercantilism, Free trade, capitalism, and so on. The evolution of modern democracies. As Heraclitus said, change alone is unchanging. You can never step in the same river twice.

Elaine. And what's your response to that?

Daniel. What was Heraclitus looking at?

Elaine. I'm not sure how to answer that . . . If you look at what's going on around you, nothing stays the same from one minute to the next.

Daniel. So we have to look at something he *wasn't* looking at. Lions change from one minute to the next, from one year to the next, from one generation to the next, but what remains the same?

Elaine. The way they live. Their social organization.

Daniel. Of course. Like every species of animal we know of, their social organization is evolutionarily stable. You won't find a single naturalist or biologist who wonders if lions might have been living differently ten thousand years ago. You won't find a single naturalist or biologist who thinks, "Golly, maybe geese didn't live in flocks ten thousand years ago. Maybe wolves didn't live in packs ten thousand years ago. Maybe whales didn't live in pods ten thousand years ago."

Elaine. So there's no reason to suppose that humans weren't living in tribes ten thousand years ago.

Daniel. Or a hundred thousand years ago . . . What we've done here might be called step five of the Quinn method — though it doesn't necessarily occur fifth. We've pulled back from the focus of the original question to gain a wider vista. The historian's vista is naturally that of the historical era, in which our social organizations have been more or less in constant flux . . . You understand that every species of animal evolves within a social organization. They don't evolve as individuals and then get together and start trying out social organizations.

Elaine. Yes . . . but you indicated that humans might have experimented with variations on the tribe.

Daniel. They might have. We have no evidence either way. But if they did, those experiments didn't survive. What survived is what we saw in place all over the world when we finally went looking — in the Americas, in Australia, in Africa, and so on. The tribe. To suppose that humans in those regions just recently began living in tribes is as silly as supposing that bees just recently began living in hives.

Elaine [doubtfully]. I see that . . .

Daniel. But . . . ?

Elaine. But I'd like to get back to something I brought up earlier. How you do what you do in your books.

Daniel [after some thought]. I've talked about some specific bits of received wisdom that I've challenged in my books, and I could talk about others. But the question I'm asked — and the question I'm trying to answer in this conversation — is not "How do you come up with these books?" but rather "How do you come up with these strange ideas?" The way I come up with my books is very much the way all authors come up with their books.

Elaine. Okay, I see that. But I have a question of my own that I think is relevant.

Daniel. Go ahead.

Elaine. As far as I'm concerned, the most original thing in *Ishmael* is your reinterpretation of the Genesis stories of the Fall and the murder of Abel. I hope you won't be offended if I ask if that was original to you.

Daniel. I'm not at all offended, and the question has been asked before. The answer is yes, it was original to me.

Elaine. Can I ask how you came up with it?

Daniel. Certainly. I came up with it using the method I've already described. First, the alertness to nonsense. The specific piece of nonsense that nagged at me was this: that the Agricultural Revolution is judged in our culture to be humanity's greatest blessing, while in Genesis it's judged to be a curse, the punishment meted out by God after the Fall. How is it possible for these two judgments to exist side by side in our culture without anyone noticing that they're contradictory?

Following my usual protocol, I pulled back to look at the matter from a wider point of view. For what sin was Adam being punished? He was being punished for eating the fruit of a tree specifically forbidden to him: the Tree of the Knowledge of Good and Evil. This gave me another bit of nonsense to think about. In our culture our possession of the knowledge of good and evil is taken for granted: It's a fine thing, a wonderful thing. Why on earth would it be forbidden? If we translate it as "knowing the difference between right and wrong," it's the very measure of human sanity.

I'd never seen a gloss on "the Knowledge of Good and Evil" that made any sense. In *The Dragons of Eden*, Carl Sagan proposed the silly idea that it was intelligence itself, which simply turns the story into nonsense.* How could God make a creature intelligent enough to understand his commands and then punish him for acquiring intelligence? Most exegetes treat "the Knowledge of Good and Evil" as a sort of placeholder. God had to forbid Adam *something*, and it doesn't matter that it makes no sense to a people to whom possession of that knowledge is counted a supreme blessing.

Pulling back still farther, I went looking into the geography of the matter and found that the Agricultural Revolution began among the Caucasians, who lived directly north of the Semites. This meant that the account of the origins of agriculture found in Genesis didn't originate among our cultural ancestors, the

---

* From the chapter "Eden as a Metaphor": "It is interesting that it is not the getting of *any* sort of knowledge that God forbids, but, specifically the knowledge of the difference between good and evil — that is, abstract and moral judgments..." Carl Sagan, *The Dragons of Eden* (New York: Random House, 1971).

Caucasians, because, of course, Genesis is a Hebrew, Semitic, text. Pulling back again, in a different direction, I looked again at the story of Cain and Abel and conceived the theory that the two of them were not individuals but rather allegorical figures, Cain representing the Caucasian agriculturalists of the north and Abel representing the Semitic herders of the south.

If this made sense as a hypothesis (and it did to me), then Cain's murder of Abel represented not a single deadly attack by one individual on another but a border war: Caucasian farmers were taking Semitic land to turn it into farmland just the way European farmers — the cultural descendants of these Caucasians — would later take Indian land to turn it into farmland. If my reading of this was correct, then the story of the Fall becomes a kind of "explaining" story, and what needed explaining was the extraordinary behavior of their neighbors to the north. Assuming that these Caucasians were practicing the same kind of agriculture that their cultural descendants practiced for the next ten thousand years to the present moment, how *were* they behaving?

Elaine. They were behaving as if the world belonged to them.

Daniel. Yes . . . But I'm trying to understand the explanation the Semites provided. According to them, these people had eaten the fruit of a tree of knowledge that was forbidden to Adam — to Man. What knowledge would God naturally want to protect, to put off limits to Man?

Elaine. His own knowledge. The knowledge he uses to rule the world.

Daniel. And why would this be the knowledge of good and evil?

Elaine. Because — and at this point I'm basically just reciting — in ruling the world, everything God does is good for one but evil for another — of necessity. As you put it, if the hunting fox gets the quail, then this is good for the fox but evil for the quail. But if the quail escapes the fox, then this is good for the quail and evil for the fox.

Daniel. And only God knows whether the fox should catch the quail or the quail should escape.

Elaine. Yes. Only God knows who should live and who should die.

Daniel. But what about those who practice agriculture the way we do?

Elaine. They act as if they've eaten at God's own tree of wisdom and know who should live and who should die. If wolves are attacking your cattle, then the wolves should die and the cattle should live. If foxes are eating your chickens, then the foxes should die and the chickens should live.

Daniel. And having taken this knowledge into their own hands, it made sense that God would condemn them to live by the sweat of their brows. They'd formerly lived an easy life, simply letting God rule the world and taking what he gave them. If they weren't content with that and wanted to rule the world themselves, then they were going to have to do all the work that God had formerly done for them. Formerly, they'd just taken whatever God planted for them. Now, having displaced God as the ruler of the world, they were going to have to plant their own food. To Cain, the tillers of the soil, planting their own food seemed like a blessing, just as it does to us. To Abel it seemed like a punishment. To us, the Agricultural Revolution seems like a technological event and a triumph. To the Semites, it seemed like a spiritual event and a catastrophe.

Elaine. Yes.

Daniel. I might add this as a footnote. I believe it was in his autobiography — though it may have been in one of his speeches — that Malcolm X identified the white race as Satan. I knew at the time I read it that this was the wrong mythological connection. Only later did I realize it would be much more appropriate to identify the white race as Cain, sweeping across the world to water his fields with the blood of his brothers.

Elaine. Well, this *has* largely been the occupation of the white race.

Daniel [after a pause]. So what do you think? Was this a useful exercise for you?

Elaine. Yes. It was useful to me to see the "method" being applied to a large, complex problem like this.

Daniel. I'm still inclined to think it will be more illuminating for readers to see you struggling to apply it right now in living color than for them to see me talking about applying it twenty years ago.

Saturday: Afternoon

Daniel. Here's a question I've received in many different forms: "Mr. Quinn, I'd like to know if you walk or ride a bicycle to work, if you use electricity, if you have central heating and air-conditioning."

Elaine. Uh-huh.

Daniel. What do you think this person is really getting at?

Elaine. I'd say he wants to know whether you practice what you preach.

Daniel. He suspects I may be a hypocrite.

Elaine. Yes.

Daniel. What assumption is at the base of all this?

Elaine. That what you preach is . . . He has his own assumptions about how to go about saving the world. We need to give up driving automobiles and walk to work. We need to turn off the electricity. Things like that.

Daniel. He has his own assumptions, and . . .

Elaine. And he figures that, if you want to save the world, then you must share them. You must be advocating the same things he advocates.

Daniel. And have I ever advocated such things?

Elaine. Not that I know of.

Daniel. I haven't. It isn't that such things would be useless, I just haven't anywhere prescribed them, because most people are already aware of them. So really his question boils down to, "Mr. Quinn, do you practice what I *expect* you to preach?"

Elaine. That's right.

Daniel. And what *do* I preach?

Elaine. Well . . . again, I'm just reciting. I think the clearest statement of it is this: If there are still people here in two hundred years, they won't be thinking the way we think, because if people go on thinking the way we think, then they'll go on *living* the way we live — and if people go on living the way we live, there won't *be* any people here in two hundred years.

Daniel. In other words, my books don't contain lists of do's and don'ts. My books are about changing minds.

Elaine. Yes.

Daniel. A lot of people find this hard to stomach. They put it this way: "I know things are screwed up, but changing minds just isn't enough."

Elaine. What do *they* think would be enough?

Daniel. That's a question for you to answer, of course.

Elaine. I'd say they want to see some *action*. Changing minds doesn't seem like action to them.

Daniel. And what likely seems like action to them?

Elaine. Well . . . passing new laws would probably count as action.

Daniel. I'd think so. What laws?

Elaine. That I don't know. Stricter environmental laws.

Daniel. In the case of the US, which branch of the government enforces the laws?

Elaine. The executive.

Daniel. And if you happen to have a chief executive like George W. Bush who doesn't give a damn about the environment?

Elaine. Then stricter laws are going to be ignored or repealed.

Daniel. And who put George Bush in office?

Elaine. People who don't give a damn about the environment. People with unchanged minds.

Daniel. So . . .

Elaine. That's the general rule. Passing new laws only helps if the electorate really wants to see them enforced.

Daniel. So sending letters to your legislators demanding change — which can also be counted as action — isn't going to do much good, either.

Elaine. No.

Daniel. What are some other things that count as action?

Elaine [after some thought]. There's protest.

Daniel. And what exactly is there to protest?

Elaine. The World Trade Organization is pretty popular.

Daniel. Do you think these questioners would consider protesting the World Trade Organization to be "enough"?

Elaine. Enough to do what?

Daniel. Well, since they're writing to me, what do you think they mean by "enough"?

Elaine. I guess I'd have to say . . . saving the human future.

Daniel. I'd agree.

Elaine. And protesting the WTO isn't going to do that.

Daniel. So how do you protest the things that put the human future in doubt? Who do you protest *to*?

Elaine. I don't know. The people around you. People in general.

Daniel. How do you organize a protest like that?

Elaine. I have no idea.

Daniel. I know of one recent instance in which protest was effective — the protest against the war in Vietnam. But what made that effective?

Elaine. I'm afraid I don't know that period very well.

Daniel. At the foundation of the movement to end the war were "teach-ins" designed to change the way people thought about the war — as opposed to the way the government wanted them to think about it. The heart of the movement was changing minds.

Elaine. And also the target was very well defined. They knew who to protest to and about what in a very exact way.

Daniel. That's right. What are some other forms of action?

Elaine. There's the Greenpeace style of action. And Earth First.

Daniel. Yes. Fighting the existing reality . . . One of the things that people often complain about changing minds is that it takes too long. Greenpeace has been at its work for thirty years, and they've certainly achieved some good results, but all the things they work against are still going on. But no one complains that what they're doing "takes too long."

Elaine. Because it's perceived to be *action.* Action doesn't have to *work.*

Daniel. That's a very astute observation — the observation of a Martian anthropologist. Expand on that.

Elaine. Well . . . the War on Drugs doesn't work — everybody knows that. We've spent billions on it, maybe trillions, but that's okay. It's action.

Daniel. In a speech I made to the Minnesota Social Investment Forum in 1993 I proposed passing legislation that would temporarily suspend present drug laws, say for three years. If we didn't like the results, we wouldn't have to do anything. The drug laws would automatically go back into effect.

Elaine. That makes sense.

Daniel. What do you think would be the result of that action?

Elaine. It wouldn't end drug use.

Daniel. Neither has the War on Drugs.

Elaine. True . . . Let's see . . . The illegal drug trade would end almost immediately, as soon as the legitimate drug companies were ready to take it over . . . You'd have to have age limits, of course.

Daniel. So some illegal trade would continue, just as it does with alcohol and tobacco.

Elaine. It probably wouldn't be as organized as it is now. I mean, kids manage to get cigarettes and booze pretty easily if they want them.

Daniel. In any case, we'd have three years to study the results. If things got worse, we'd just let the drug laws automatically go back into effect. Or if things seemed to be getting better, we could extend the suspension for another three years and see what happens.

Elaine. It makes too much sense ever to be adopted.

Daniel. On the other hand, Prohibition — the War on Alcohol — was eventually abandoned.

Elaine. True . . . But drinking was always more . . . mainstream. I mean, drinking itself wasn't criminalized, was it?

Daniel. No, I never heard of anyone doing hard time for having a drink. It was just illegal to manufacture, sell, transport, or import the stuff.

Elaine. Uh-huh.

Daniel. Despite its long history of failure, this belief in the effectiveness of action runs deep in our culture. Enacting the Eighteenth Amendment, the amendment that instituted Prohibition, was *action*, and it was cheered by tens of millions. The fact that it not only failed to produce a sober nation but gave drinking a new cachet and encouraged the rise of a vast new criminal enterprise didn't dampen anyone's enthusiasm for action. After World War Two, Communism came to be perceived as the greatest threat ever faced by this nation. This called for action. The public loved the witch hunt instigated by the House Un-American Activities Committee, especially when it produced a Hollywood blacklist of famous actors, directors, and writers whose films were in fact no more subversive of "American" values than any others.

Elaine. I've heard of it, though it was before my time, obviously.

Daniel. But of course that was very minor action compared with the trillions of dollars the government spent to thwart the spread of Communism and hopefully bring down the Soviet Union. Forty-odd years of action, action, action. Then, suddenly, the Soviet Union simply dissolved — not because of any action undertaken by our government, but because the minds of the Soviet people had changed. They were fed up with the lives their government had given them. The greatest Communist experiment of all time had failed, and the spread of Communism ceased to seem like much of a threat — again, through no action taken by our government.

Elaine. Then came the War on Drugs.

Daniel. More trillions spent, and no sign of victory anywhere. But plenty of action.

Elaine. I'd say that some environmental legislation produced good results.

Daniel. Yet we've reelected a president who's made it clear that he doesn't give a damn about protecting the environment. What's this mean?

Elaine. That the voters who put him in office don't give a damn, either.

Daniel. When will they start giving a damn?

Elaine. When they starting thinking a new way.

Daniel. So it always comes back to that. It doesn't do much good to have the laws in place unless we elect a chief executive who wants to execute them.

Elaine. True.

Daniel. Here's another way to look at this. Action proceeds automatically from vision. I mean that if a certain vision is in place, you don't have to "take action" to realize it. For example, if the American people didn't want to drink alcohol, the Eighteenth Amendment wouldn't have been needed, would it?

Elaine. No. They would just have stopped drinking. Then the manufacturers would've stopped making it and the importers would've stopped importing it.

Daniel. But in fact they didn't want to stop drinking, so passing the Eighteenth Amendment was futile: It wasn't supported by the prevalent vision. Similarly, they don't want to stop using drugs like marijuana, cocaine, and heroin, so the War on Drugs is just as futile. This is certainly, at least in part, what Buckminster Fuller meant when he said, "You never change things by fighting the existing reality." The existing reality hasn't changed a particle since the war began. Except, that is, for the worse. Just speaking from personal experience, the only drugs I saw being used by kids in my school days were nicotine and booze.

Elaine. That's certainly changed.

Daniel. By far the biggest action of the last three centuries has been the Industrial Revolution, and that was driven entirely by vision. I assume you know what that vision was.

Elaine. Yes. Again just reciting, people began to see that they could get ahead by inventing new things, developing new processes — or improving on old ones.

Daniel. No one had to "take action" to make it happen — no one had to pass laws requiring people to be inventive.

Elaine. It was in their own interest to be inventive.

Daniel. But you understand that the Industrial Revolution couldn't have started during the Middle Ages.

Elaine. No, the vision wasn't there. It only came into existence as a result of the Renaissance and the scientific revolution it ushered in.

Daniel [after a short break]. What do you know about hypnotism?

Elaine. Hypnotism? That's quite a change of subject

Daniel. Yes.

Elaine. What do I know about it . . . ? Nothing more than is generally known.

Daniel. What would you say is generally known?

Elaine. Golly . . . I'd say that "known" is probably too strong a word. *[Thinks about it for a while.]* The impression you get from hypnotism in the movies is that it induces a trance state in which the subject is highly suggestible and can be given instructions that will be carried out after being brought out of hypnosis. Supposedly.

Daniel. Supposedly?

Elaine. I think there's some doubt — among those qualified to have doubts — that hypnotism actually exists. The hypnotic state may just be something the subject unconsciously adopts to please the hypnotist.

Daniel. Yes, that's a fair statement.

Elaine. It strikes me as being unprovable either way.

Daniel. That was true for a long time, but recent brain-imaging studies seem to suggest that there really is a hypnotic state that is quite distinct from the ordinary. I'll have to back up and take a running start at this . . . When your eye encounters photons bouncing off an apple, they're turned into a pattern that's sent to the primary visual cortex. There, the general shape of the apple is recognized and sent on to a higher region of brain function where its color is identified. Then this pattern moves along to a still-higher region where it's put together with other knowledge that enables you to recognize that this is an apple, not a strawberry. This bottom-to-top flow of data is what we think of as the ordinary process of perception.

Elaine. Uh-huh.

Daniel. But there is also a top-to-bottom flow of information that is equally powerful, and it's a curious fact that the neural paths carrying information down to the bottom outnumber paths carrying information up to the top ten to one.

Elaine. That *is* strange.

Daniel. It's a commonplace that to Western eyes all Orientals look alike — and vice versa. If you and a Korean are presented with two Oriental faces, the same photons will reach both of your eyes, but what you and the Korean will actually end up perceiving will be very different. You'll very likely be struck by their similarities, while the Korean observer will be struck by their differences. For example, he'll be able to tell you whether the two individuals are Korean, Chinese, or Japanese. The Korean will notice the characteristics that distinguish one face from the other, whereas he would probably fail to see the characteristics that distinguish one Caucasian face from another.

Elaine. I see what you're saying. A lifetime of experience outweighs what the eyes are taking in.

Daniel. An exotic insect in a photograph might strike you as something repulsive, but it would strike an entomologist in an entirely different way.

Elaine. Uh-huh.

Daniel. In Nazi concentration camps the same images reached the eyes of the prisoners and the guards, but the guards, conditioned by decades of anti-Semitism, no longer saw humans when they looked at Jews, they saw vermin that deserved to be exterminated. In other words, the top level of perception overruled the bottom level, so that they were able to do their killing without feelings of guilt or remorse. The Stockholm syndrome is probably an example of the same effect.

Elaine. Remind me what that is.

Daniel. Hostages cease to see their captors as enemies and identify them as allies.

Elaine. Yeah.

Daniel. Faith healing represents another example. A famous
case is that of one Helen Sullivan, who suffered from a cancer
that had weakened her spine to such an extent that she spent
most of her time in a wheelchair and could only walk with the
support of a brace. In fact, she hadn't been without the brace
for four months when she attended a "Miracle Service" held by
Kathryn Kuhlman, a practitioner of the "shotgun" technique of
faith healing, which consists of announcing that someone in the
audience is *being* cured of something — rather than inviting
someone up *to be* cured.

Mrs. Sullivan, hearing that someone was "being" cured of
cancer, was sure it was her. She hobbled from her wheelchair
to the stage, tore off her brace, and ran back and forth across
the stage several times, then returned to her wheelchair, waving
her brace in the air. A few hours later, in the middle of the
night, she woke up in terrible pain. X-rays revealed that a
cancer-weakened vertebra had collapsed, presumably as a
result of the strain she'd placed on it running back and forth
across the stage. Two months later she died.

Elaine. Uh-huh. Her "faith" at the top overruled the pain she
would have otherwise felt during the demonstration.

Daniel. So it would seem. Hypnosis appears to initiate a similar
top-down overruling of what is perceived at the bottom level. At
least this is what a recent experiment seems to indicate. A neuro-
scientist at Columbia University put a group of subjects known
to be highly susceptible to hypnosis together with a group known
to be highly resistant to hypnosis, took them all through the

process of hypnotic induction, then gave them these instructions: "Soon, when you're no longer under hypnosis, you're going to be playing a computer game inside a brain scanner. Here's the game. On the computer monitor you're going to see sets of meaningless squiggles that will look like words written in a foreign alphabet. Your job is not to try to make out what these mean, because they're just gibberish. Your job is just to identify the *color* of the squiggles — red, green, blue, or yellow — and press a button of the corresponding color as quickly as possible."

Elaine. Okay.

Daniel. The catch is that the squiggles on the screen were *not* meaningless squiggles. They were perfectly readable English words — *red, green, blue,* and *yellow* in bold type — and the color of the type didn't necessarily match the words. The word *red* might be colored blue, the word *yellow* might be colored green, and so on.

Elaine. I see.

Daniel. What the experiment showed was this. The group that was highly susceptible to hypnosis identified the colors of the words significantly faster than the group that was highly resistant to hypnosis. I'm sure you can see why.

Elaine. Yes. If you see the word *yellow* — assuming you're literate — you're going to think "yellow" first, regardless of the word's color. You're going to have to think again to see that the word is written in green.

Daniel. Exactly. But the subjects who were highly hypnotizable manifestly *didn't* see the word *yellow.* They saw meaningless squiggles and so were able to push the green button without hesitation.

Elaine. Interesting.

Daniel. And you're wondering what the hell this has to do with anything.

Elaine [laughs]. Yes, I have to admit that I am.

Daniel. The person who brought this experiment to my attention remarked that it put him in mind of Mother Culture.

Elaine. Uh-huh.

Daniel says nothing.

Elaine [after a minute]. And?

Daniel. And you're a Martian anthropologist in training.

Elaine [after spending some time in thought]. I don't see the question.

Daniel. This morning you expressed some dissatisfaction with a diet that consists entirely of questions.

Elaine [laughs nervously]. Yes, that's true. I guess I should say that I don't see the problem.

Daniel. I didn't say there was a problem. I just presented you with a statement.

Elaine. And what was it again?

Daniel. My friend said that everything I've just told you put him in mind of Mother Culture.

Elaine. What did he mean exactly?

Daniel. That's all he said. He didn't elaborate on it.

Elaine. What do *you* think he meant?

Daniel. You don't think you can figure it out?

Elaine [after some thought]. He meant that Mother Culture hypnotizes us, influences us in a way that makes the top level of our perceptions overrule the bottom level, what's actually before our eyes.

Daniel. Yes, I'm sure that was more or less what he had in mind.

Elaine. So?

Daniel. So you're in training as a Martian anthropologist.

Elaine groans.

Daniel. Look, Elaine. You were saying that in your day-to-day life, people don't ask you direct questions like the ones I get from my readers. That's absolutely true. It's also true for me. Things don't come out of the air with tags attached saying, "Something for the Martian anthropologist to examine." The Martian anthropologist in me is always awake. It's habitual for me to examine *whatever* comes my way — and I'm trying to make it habitual for you. When you leave here, there's not going to be anyone around to point out things you need to look at.

Elaine. I know that.

Daniel. So.

Elaine. I guess the problem is that this person's statement seems so . . . innocuous. Even obvious. Don't you think?

Daniel says nothing.

Elaine sighs. In the end, calling Mother Culture a hypnotist is just a metaphor, isn't it?

Daniel. Shall we take a break while you think about it?

Elaine. Yes.

Elaine [an hour later]. I think I've gotten somewhere.

Daniel. Good.

Elaine. It seems to me that the issue is not the act of hypnosis itself. You've already mentioned instances in which top-down thinking rules, in the absence of any actual act of hypnosis. The Stockholm syndrome is one example. I thought of another. In Australia, aboriginal witch doctors employ a magical tactic called pointing the bone, which can literally bring death to an enemy who accepts the reality of the curse. Are you familiar with that?

Daniel. Yes.

Elaine. Pointing the bone doesn't involve any hypnotic act, but it achieves the effect of an hypnotic act, in which the bottom level of thinking is overruled by the top.

Daniel. Uh-huh.

Elaine. In *Ishmael* you described the story Mother Culture tells us as the driving force of our culture. For example, she tells us that the world is a human possession, and when we look at the world, that's exactly what we see. Even though, as a practical matter — as a matter of reality — we know full well that we have no deed to the world signed by God.

Daniel. Uh-huh.

Elaine. Our cultural conditioning at the top level overrules the bottom level.

Daniel. Uh-huh.

Elaine. If it's valid to think of top-down thinking operating on concentration-camp guards and on hostages in the Stockholm syndrome, then it's valid to think of top-down thinking operating on us on a very wide scale.

Daniel. Uh-huh.

Elaine. So your friend's observation seems completely valid to me. Although there's no specific or single act of hypnotism, the constant hum of Mother Culture's voice in our ears from the cradle on up causes us to overrule the raw evidence of our senses. In our own way, as we go about the task of devouring the world, we're like those concentration-camp guards. They viewed exterminating Jews as just something that had to be done. At the bottom, they were aware that other nations would regard what they were doing as profoundly wicked, but this awareness was overruled by their cultural conditioning at the top. We're similarly aware — at the bottom — that other peoples and our own descendants are going to view our destruction of the world as profoundly wicked, but this awareness is overruled by our cultural conditioning at the top, which tells us that this is just something that has to be done. It's a job, like exterminating Jews.

Daniel. Uh-huh.

Elaine [after waiting awhile for Daniel to continue]. So?

Daniel. So, what?

Elaine [laughs]. I guess I'm waiting for a grade.

Daniel. In other words, you think you're finished.

Elaine. Is there more?

Daniel. If there was more, how would you go about seeing it?

Elaine. Oh . . . I'd pull back and look at the matter from a higher angle.

Daniel. That's the procedure. What is it you see by pulling back and looking at things from a higher angle?

Elaine. I'd say . . . more ground.

Daniel. Of course.

Elaine. Okay. *[After a few minutes.]* Okay, here's what I see . . . Your friend was referring to *our* Mother Culture. At least I assume so.

Daniel. So do I.

Elaine. But *every* culture has a Mother Culture who hums in everyone's ears from the cradle up.

Daniel. Of course.

Elaine. I even supplied an example of my own. The Mother Culture of Australia's aborigines tells them, among other things, that their witch doctors wield immense occult powers.

Daniel. That's right. Among many other thousands or millions of things, just like our Mother Culture. When my hard drive failed a few months ago I lost a very significant quote from, I believe, the chief of a northwestern American tribe. He said, approximately — referring to us, of course — "It didn't occur to us that you meant to *stay*." Their top-level cultural conditioning told them that people don't just move into someone else's territory and settle down as if it were their own, and this overruled what their eyes were telling them.

Elaine. Yes, that's very clear.

Daniel. And now what do you think of the apparently odd fact that downward neural paths outnumber upward paths ten to one?

Elaine [after some thought]. I think it means that humans are hardwired for culture.

Daniel. Yes, I think so, too. We evolved as cultural beings, and cultural conditioning at the top level serves to tell us how to evaluate and act on the information we receive from the bottom level — a much more complex task for us than it is for squirrels or sharks.

Elaine. Though what this conditioning tells us is not always . . . reliable.

Daniel. That's true — and that's one reason why it's worth examining. The cultural conditioning of Native Americans told them we didn't mean to stay — couldn't possibly mean to stay. Our cultural conditioning tells us that the way we live is the way humans were meant to live from the beginning of time and that we have to hold on to this way of living even if it kills us.

Sunday: Morning

Elaine. I feel bad that this has to be our last day.

Daniel. Why is that?

Elaine. I'm sure we could go on this way for weeks.

Daniel. I wish you were right. The fact is I've run out of questions that seem worth exploring. I've gone over the hundreds I have on hand a dozen times.

Elaine. That's hard to believe.

Daniel. They're just very straightforward. Have no hidden depths, present no challenge.

Elaine [alarmed]. Does that mean we're finished?

Daniel [laughs]. Oh no. We have a question we left unanswered from the first day, and then I've saved a really munchy problem till last.

Elaine. Good. What's the question we left unanswered?

Daniel. We were talking about why the first three million years of human life had been swept under the rug by the people of our culture.

Elaine. Oh yeah.

Daniel. We'd gotten to the fact that these three million years pose a threat to the understanding of ourselves that informs our cultural mythology. Care to summarize?

Elaine. Let me think ... According to our cultural mythology, we and we alone are humanity. To acknowledge that our ancient ancestors have any claim to humanity — to acknowledge that their lives amounted to anything — is obviously a threat to that mythology. The way we live is the way humans were meant to live from the beginning, and our ancient ancestors were just passing the time, accomplishing nothing. Truly human life didn't start until we came along to begin building civilization.

Daniel. Very good. And you remember I said there was an even more dangerous threat involved in acknowledging the first three million years of human life.

Elaine. Yes...

Daniel. Are you ready to tackle that now?

Elaine. I should've been thinking about it...

Daniel says nothing.

Elaine. I remember I asked some question you didn't want to answer, but I don't remember what it was. It must have been relevant.

Daniel. What should you be doing now?

Elaine. Backing off. Trying to get a higher, wider view of the terrain.

Daniel says nothing.

Elaine [after a minute]. I remember what it was now. I asked who would feel threatened. Actually . . . Okay, this might be useful. What I'm thinking about is the period when people were being compelled to consider the possibility that humans were not the product of a special act of creation that occurred just a few thousand years ago. That was obviously a very distressing idea to a lot of people . . . But we already knew that.

Daniel. Take your time.

Elaine. But it was especially distressing to . . . Christian thinkers.

Daniel [after a minute]. Maybe it would help to come at the problem from a different angle.

Elaine. What angle?

Daniel. What are some of the things we've done before that have been helpful?

Elaine. Well, there was turning the tables.

Daniel. Try anything.

Elaine [sighing]. Turning the tables . . . What would that mean here?

Daniel says nothing.

Elaine. Here was the setup. "We detest the idea that humans were not the product of a special creation just a few thousand years ago." Instead of trying to call up evidence to change their minds, I'm going to ask why this is so detestable. Why don't you say, "Hurray! The human family is vastly larger and older than we thought!" Why aren't you cheering instead of grousing?

Daniel. Uh-huh.

Elaine. What do you find so disturbing about the idea that we've been here for three million years?

Daniel says nothing.

Elaine [after thinking for a couple of minutes]. I've got it, I think. If we've been around for three million years, where was God all this time? Now, *that's* a dangerous question.

Daniel. I'd say so.

Elaine. I think I see it now. We are humanity, therefore our religions are the *religions* of humanity. But our religions are only three or four thousand years old — Christianity only two thousand years old. So how can these be considered the religions of humanity if humanity is three million years old? That just doesn't make sense.

Daniel says nothing.

Elaine. It was okay when that bishop's date was in place. What was it?

Daniel. It was 4004 BC. According to Bishop Ussher's calculation, Adam and Eve, along with the rest of the universe, came into existence almost exactly six thousand years ago.

Elaine. And that was okay, because . . . Because that meant that God began to interact with humanity right from the start, from the very first day. The whole biblical story was safe . . . How did Ussher make his calculation?

Daniel. Basically he added up the ages provided in Old Testament genealogies, which can be traced right up into the historical period — up to the first destruction of the Temple in

Jerusalem, in fact. I don't recall how he determined the date of this event, but after that it was just simple arithmetic.

Elaine. I see. But in any case, this puts the notion that Christianity is humanity's religion on a solid footing, generation after generation and event by event right from the beginning. That's what you lose if you toss out Ussher's date — that foundation.

Daniel. Yes, so it would seem.

Elaine. But it occurs to me that the only religionists outraged by losing humanity's special creation were — and are — Christians. I've never heard of any outrage among Jews or Buddhists over it.

Daniel. And where does that lead you?

Elaine. I'm not sure . . . I guess it leads me here: Christianity is the only one of our religions that actually represents itself as a religion for the whole of humanity. Judaism and Hinduism are both specifically ethnic religions, wouldn't you say? I mean, Judaism is for Jews and Hinduism is for the people of India.

Daniel. It seems clear enough that Judaism is for Jews, since they are a specifically Chosen people. I'm not aware of any evangelical tendency among Hindus.

Elaine. But what about Islam?

Daniel. Offhand, it does seem to be represented as a religion of the whole of humanity. Let me check a source. *[Returning twenty minutes later.]* This is from *The World's Religions*, by J. N. D. Anderson: "There can be little doubt that Muhammad at first believed that he had only to proclaim his message to gain Jewish support, for was not his message the one, true religion preached by Abraham and all the patriarchs and prophets, ever corrupted only to be proclaimed anew?"

Elaine. Um. That shoots my theory.

Daniel. What was your theory?

Elaine. Maybe it doesn't. Islam's book is the Koran, not the Bible.

Daniel. And so?

Elaine. And so they're not tied to the creation account in Genesis — or to Bishop Ussher's date for creation. Or at least not as tied as the Christians, who were upset by losing that foundation that enabled them to trace their roots back to the beginning of human life.

Daniel. That seems plausible. But I'm still not sure what point you're reaching for.

Elaine [laughing]. By this time, I'm not quite sure myself.

Daniel. Let's take a little break and maybe it'll come to you.

Elaine. Okay.

Daniel [half an hour later]. Any luck?

Elaine. No. I think I reached my point and then overshot it. You can skip this part of the dialogue when you do the book.

Daniel. Not at all. I wouldn't dream of it. You did brilliantly. And you made some points that I missed in a lecture I delivered on this subject at Southwestern University* a few years ago.

---

*Georgetown, Texas. See appendix 2.

Elaine. Huh. I guess that's something to brag about.

Daniel. It is. So . . . Anything to add?

Elaine. You mean to this particular subject? No.

Daniel. Are you ready to move on to something completely different?

Elaine. Sure.

Daniel. Good. While on tour for *The Holy* in the fall of 2002 I happened to see a billboard showing some golfers and displaying the message "Golfers Against Cancer."

Elaine. Uh-huh.

Daniel says nothing.

Elaine. That's it?

Daniel. That's it. Right out of the air, about sixty feet above the ground, by the expressway. Just the thing for a Martian anthropologist.

Elaine. Lord. Golfers against cancer. That's all?

Daniel. That's all.

Elaine. Why golfers?

Daniel. The organization was founded in 1997. As of today they've raised more than seven million dollars for cancer research.

Elaine. But why *golfers*?

Daniel. Are you asking *me*?

Elaine. No, not really. It's just my first question. Wasn't it yours?

Daniel. I'm afraid I don't remember. It may have been. If you see something there to explore, explore it.

Elaine. Do you know what motivated the thing?

Daniel. I believe it was founded in support of a golf pro with cancer. I don't know the details.

Elaine [after thinking for a time]. Would it be different if it were dentists against cancer, or hairdressers? Of course it would.

Daniel says nothing.

Elaine. I guess there's nothing really there in that line of questioning, beyond the obvious.

Daniel says nothing.

Elaine. Golfers *Against* Cancer. As if it were an issue, like abortion or capital punishment. As if there might be another organization, Golfers *For* Cancer . . . I guess the expected reaction to this initiative is supposed to be "Hooray for golfers!" But *everyone's* against cancer, aren't they? It makes you wonder why film stars, lawyers, baseball players, prizefighters, and tennis pros haven't also come together against cancer. What are they waiting for?

Daniel says nothing.

Elaine. I'm really floundering here.

Daniel. Don't be so hard on yourself. You've only had it for a minute.

Elaine. Lord . . . Golfers Against Cancer . . .

Daniel. What should you be doing now?

Elaine. Pulling back. Trying to get a wider view.

Daniel. Right.

Elaine [sighing]. Golfers Against Cancer . . . Why not Parkinson's or muscular dystrophy?

Daniel says nothing.

Elaine [after thinking it over]. There's nothing in that . . . I think I should take a walk. I just feel too much pressure with you sitting here waiting for me to come up with something.

Daniel. Yes, that's probably a good idea.

Elaine [about an hour later]. Can I use your computer to do some research?

Daniel. Of course.

Elaine. I may need to make some notes.

Daniel. Grab a sheet from my printer.

Elaine [three-quarters of an hour later]. I have no idea where this will go.

Daniel. That's how it works. You pick a starting point and see where it goes.

Elaine. It started with my question about Parkinson's and muscular dystrophy. Or maybe it didn't. I don't know . . .

Daniel. Go ahead.

Elaine. What I wondered was this: What would these golfers say if I asked them if God is against cancer. My guess is that they'd say yes. What do you think?

Daniel. You can figure that out.

Elaine [sighing]. Well, people in general — or believers in general — certainly pray to God to cure them of illnesses. This means...

Daniel [after a minute]. Yes?

Elaine. This means there's an assumption of sidedness. Believers have to assume that God is against cancer.

Daniel. Okay.

Elaine. If the answer is yes, God's against cancer, I'd next ask if he's also against plague, AIDS, HIV, anthrax, polio, rabies, measles, and all the thousands of other diseases we suffer from.

Daniel. Smallpox, tetanus, pneumonia, scarlet fever, typhoid fever.

Elaine Yes, I've got all those and dozens more *[referring to a list she's holding].* Anthrax, meningitis, cowpox, croup, botulism, Lyme disease, brucellosis, yellow fever, ebola hemorrhagic fever, cholera, necrotizing fasciitis — that's the "flesh-eating disease" that's so much fun — dysentery, tuberculosis, mononucleosis, diphtheria, mumps, glanders, influenza, leprosy, herpes, Legionnaire's disease, gonorrhea, leptospirosis, hepatitis, listeriosis, peritonitis, and on and on. Okay. Now what causes all these diseases? Viruses, bacteria, and fungi. I think that's it.

Daniel. It is, as far as I know.

Elaine. Anyway . . . If God is against all these diseases, then he must surely be against all the fungi, bacteria, and viruses that cause them.

Daniel. That makes sense.

Elaine. And if he's against these fungi, bacteria, and viruses, then it seems logical that he has to be against all the creatures that can injure or kill us with a bite or a sting — black widow spiders, scorpions, mosquitoes, tarantulas . . .

Daniel. Bees, wasps, brown recluse spiders . . .

Elaine. Rattlesnakes, coral snakes, copperheads, cottonmouths, cobras . . .

Daniel. Green mambas, bushmasters, pythons, puff adders . . .

Elaine. Barracudas, sharks . . .

Daniel. Jellyfish, stingrays. Not to mention lions, tigers, grizzly bears, and wolves.

Elaine. Right. And then there are all the parasites and plants that are deadly or harmful to us. *[Reading from her list.]* Roundworms, pinworms, hookworms, flukes, tapeworms, whipworms, poison ivy, acanthamoebae, monkshood, bird's-foot trefoil, black locust, death angel mushrooms, celandine, death camas, devil's trumpet, dogbane, henbane, Dutchman's-breeches, foxglove, laburnum, ragworts, mayapple, moonseed, deadly nightshade, oleander, poison hemlock, poison oak, poison sumac, pokeweed, rosary pea, skunk cabbage, purple vetch, cowbane, white snakeroot . . .

Daniel. You really went to town on those.

Elaine [laughs]. Okay . . . This is where I've got to. I said I wasn't sure where this was going, and I'm still not.

Daniel. It seems like you're building to some sort of conclusion.

Elaine. Conclusion?

Daniel. About God.

Elaine. Oh yes, of course. Since all these creatures continue to thrive, either God is *not* against them or he's extremely ineffectual in getting his way.

Daniel. So it would seem.

Elaine. But does this have anything to do with golfers being against cancer?

Daniel. It seems highly relevant to me. Relevant to the thinking behind it, which is what an anthropologist is interested in.

Elaine. Okay.

Daniel. But I don't think you've carried this as far as it'll go.

Elaine. I was afraid you'd say that.

Daniel. You've reached the middle of a profound subject.

Elaine. Which you're not going to name.

Daniel. Well, I'd rather not.

Elaine [after a minute]. I don't think it could be called the problem of evil.

Daniel. Maybe not, though it's certainly related to the problem of evil.

Elaine [after some thought]. Disappointment with God . . . I guess I thought of that because my roommate was reading a book with that title.

Daniel. You didn't read it yourself?

Elaine. No . . .

Daniel. Okay. Disappointment with God.

Elaine. "Why did God let my loved one die of _____?"

Daniel. Uh-huh. And what's the answer?

Elaine. There's more than one. "God's knowledge is superior to ours. You assume that what was best for your loved one was to go on living, but you can't know that. God does. Though you naturally can't think such a thing, it's entirely possible that your loved one was spared an even worse fate — and we all know there are fates worse than death."

Daniel. True.

Elaine. Here's another: "The death of your loved one has made you doubt God. Perhaps this is exactly the point. God is testing your faith. God tests all of us at some point in our lives, and some receive harder tests than others. Receiving a hard test is not a mark of God's disfavor but rather the opposite. It is, after all, the champions who are given the hardest tests — to swim faster, jump higher, run farther. By giving you this hardest of tests, God is giving you an opportunity to become a champion of faith."

Daniel. I spoke earlier of lined paper. What you're doing is providing the lines on the sheet titled "Disappointment with God."

Elaine. I'm not sure what you mean by "providing the lines."

Daniel. Providing the answers that go on the lines.

Elaine. I see, yes.

Daniel. There are assumptions you need to be looking at for these answers.

Elaine. God . . . I'm sure there are dozens.

Daniel. You want to break here for lunch to think about it? It's been a long morning.

Elaine. Yes, it has been.

Sunday: Afternoon

Daniel. So. You've supplied two lines on the sheet of paper headed "Why did God let my loved one die?" Now we're looking for things beneath the surface of the paper.

Elaine. There are two obvious assumptions: "God exists" and "God is good."

Daniel. Yes, those are the basics. There are other assumptions that aren't so easily seen. Can you bring them up and make them visible?

Elaine. I think so — at least some of them. "God is aware of everything that happens on earth." If this weren't so, he couldn't be held accountable for the loved one's death.

Daniel. That makes sense.

Elaine. And "God knows what causes us pain."

Daniel. Uh-huh.

Elaine. "God has a special care for us and invites us to invoke this special care when we're in trouble."

Daniel. Certainly.

Elaine. Here's where things start to get sticky. "Because God has a special care for us, he's ready to help us — to take our side — if we're attacked by a lion, a shark, a spider, a bacterium, a fungus, or a virus."

Daniel. Uh-huh.

Elaine. "He was aware that my loved one was being attacked, but ignored my pleas for help and declined to take my loved one's side against the attacker. He let me down, and so I have good reason to be disappointed in him."

Daniel. Yes, this is where things get sticky. So what do you do?

Elaine. I'm not sure what you mean.

Daniel. This is where you turn the paper around and write sideways against the lines provided.

Elaine. Hmm.

Daniel. What's written on the lines so far assumes that God has a special care for us and is "on our side" against all the thousands of species of life that can harm us. What do you write if you turn the paper sideways?

Elaine. Oh, I see. I think. Instead of supposing that he has a special care for us and is on our side against all others, we can suppose that he has a care for all living things and is not on any side.

Daniel. Which in fact appears to be the case, since sometimes "they" win and sometimes "we" win.

Elaine. Okay. And this brings to mind something you pointed out in *Ishmael*: Everything that happens in the living community is good for one but evil for another — and it can't be otherwise. If an owl snatches a mouse, then this is good for the owl but evil for the mouse. If the owl fails to snatch the mouse, then this is good for the mouse but evil for the owl.

Daniel. If there is a God, and he cares for everything that lives, then it would be absurd for him to be on the mouse's side or the owl's side.

Elaine. Exactly.

Daniel. See if you can carry on from here.

Elaine [after a few minutes of thought]. On the basis of observation alone, it seems unnecessary to imagine that every contest for life is decided by divine intervention. If the mouse is in the wrong place at the wrong time, the owl's going to win. If the mouse is alert and swift, and can reach shelter in time, then the mouse is going to win.

Daniel. Yes.

Elaine. During a flu epidemic, the virus is going to win in some cases and lose in others. Again, it seems stupid to imagine that each contest is decided by God. If the infected person is old and weak, the virus is probably going to win — but not always. If the infected person is young and healthy, the virus is probably going to lose — but not always.

Daniel [after a minute, when she doesn't continue]. Well done. You've just explained why I'm never disappointed with the gods that I prefer to people the universe with. I never expect them to take my side against others. If I come down with pneumonia, I don't expect the gods to take my side against the virus or bacterium that is pursuing its life in my body. If I travel to Indonesia, I don't expect the gods to strike dead a mosquito that is about to dine on my neck — and incidentally give me a case of malaria. If a mountain lion attacks me in the Andes, I don't expect the gods to help me kill it. If I'm swimming off the coast of Florida, I don't expect the gods to shoo away the sharks.

Elaine. That universe makes more sense to me, personally.

Daniel. Having reached this point, do you want to take on the problem of evil?

Elaine. How do you define that?

Daniel [after some thought]. If God is willing to prevent evil but unable to do so, then he's impotent. If he's able to prevent evil but not willing to, then he's corrupt. And so, since evil certainly exists, God is either impotent or corrupt and therefore cannot be God. I'd have to do some research to be sure that this is the classical definition.

Elaine. How do you define evil?

Daniel. How do *you* define it?

Elaine. Well, it obviously goes beyond disease. It would have to include natural disasters like earthquakes, hurricanes, and torna-does, as well as all the evil that humans are capable of.

Daniel. Uh huh.

Elaine [after some thought]. I'm having a hard time seeing . . . No, the problem is in the definition itself. In the terms of the definition. In effect . . . If you take this definition of the problem of evil . . . In effect, according to this definition, a good God couldn't have made the world at all or peopled it with humans. To be honest, I'm not sure what the hell I'm saying.

Daniel. Always a good sign.

Elaine [laughs and spends a few minutes thinking]. The god of the definition is a particular kind of god, one who is both omnipotent and "good" — and here that *good* is in quotes. Or one who must *be* both omnipotent and good — or he fails to qualify as God. But it seems possible to challenge that definition . . .

Daniel. Uh-huh.

Elaine. Why not a god who is just supremely *competent?* A god who has created a world that functions independently of his relentless scrutiny and control.

Daniel. Why not, indeed.

Elaine. A competent parent produces children who don't need second-by-second supervision. A competent engineer designs machines that operate without his constant oversight.

Daniel. Where does this leave the problem of evil?

Elaine. This is what I would say: The problem of evil only arises if you posit a god who is a supreme puppeteer, controlling the movement of everything he creates, down to the atomic level. This kind of god supervises the fall of every leaf, the rise and fall of every wave in the ocean. For me — and I expect for you — the problem of evil doesn't exist.

Daniel. You're right about that.

Elaine [after a couple of minutes]. I'm thinking about those golfers against cancer.

Daniel. And?

Elaine. I'm not sure what conclusion I should be drawing about them after all this.

Daniel. Who said you should be drawing some conclusion about them? They represent a cultural phenomenon that gave us something to think about. That led us to some interesting insights.

Elaine. Was your train of thought the same as mine?

Daniel. Actually, you dug up something I didn't, the point that the problem of evil only arises if you're talking about a particular kind of god.

Elaine. So I get a passing grade on the final?

Daniel. You get an A plus.

Elaine. So do you think the effort paid off? In terms of the book you hope to produce.

Daniel. I wish I had more questions of the same quality to explore.

Elaine. I don't suppose you can just make them up.

Daniel [laughs]. No, I couldn't manage that. But what about you? Did you get what you came for?

Elaine [thinks about that for a while]. Not exactly, but I got something better. What's the proverb? Give a man a fish and you feed him for a day; teach him how to fish and you feed him for a lifetime. I guess I have to say that I came looking for some fish and you taught me how to fish.

Appendix I

The New Renaissance

Address delivered at the University of Texas
Health Science Center at Houston, March 7, 2002

TWENTY-FIVE YEARS AGO, when I began working on a book
that would someday become a novel called *Ishmael*, very
few people thought humanity was in much trouble, provided the
Cold War didn't turn into a nuclear war. Everything looked fine,
to most people. That's changed around very drastically in the last
ten years — perhaps not *completely* around.

Back in 1995, when I was visiting a school in Albuquerque that
had used *Ishmael* as the year's focus book, I was asked to meet
with a very high-level group of health care professionals — the
assembled department heads of Presbyterian Health Care
Services, which functions as a regional hospital system. I
accepted the invitation but wondered what I might have to say
that was relevant to their professional concerns. I know nothing
about hospitals or health care or the medical profession. I don't
even watch *ER*.

It was clear when I sat down with them — perhaps twenty men
and women — that they'd all been deeply moved by my book. But
none of them could quite explain why it was relevant to them in

their profession. I think what it really came down to was that, as a result of reading *Ishmael*, they *themselves* had changed, simply as human beings, and they were trying to figure out how this change would or could or should change them as health care professionals.

I'm afraid I wasn't much help, but I don't think I need to apologize for this. I had no way of knowing how their professional lives needed to change; only they could know that.

I had a similar experience a year later when I was asked to address an annual conference of high-level executives involved in the design and manufacture of commercial floor-covering systems. Don't laugh. This is a multibillion-dollar global industry — and an industry that at that time was highly pollutive, a huge contributor to landfills, and totally dependent on and extremely wasteful of nonrenewable resources (petroleum, mainly).

They, too, had been profoundly changed by my work, but thereafter the similarity between the two groups ended. These people weren't in any doubt about how to translate this change into a change in their professional lives. Which is a good thing, because of course I wouldn't have had a clue. They knew what they had to change, and they'd already put into place a set of long-range goals that not only transformed their industry but compelled associated industries to change as well. In order to retain their position in this industry, giants like DuPont were literally forced to start thinking a different way themselves.

If I were asked to address a group of investment counselors or chemical engineers or airline executives — and none of these are out of the question — it'd be the same. My task would not be to tell them what changes to make in their professional lives, because I know nothing about investments or chemical engineering or airline management.

With every group, no matter what principle or profession draws it together, my task is the same: to send people home with a new and deeper insight into the central problem that draws us *all* together as humans, regardless of our occupations — and that problem is nothing less than the survival of our species.

People often ask me if I have any hope for our survival. What they really want to know, of course, is whether I can provide *them* with some grounds for hope.

I *am* hopeful, because I feel sure that something extraordinary is going to happen in your lifetime — in the lifetime of those of you who are three or four decades younger than I am. I'm talking about something much more extraordinary than has happened in *my* lifetime, which has included the birth of television, the splitting of the atom, space travel, and instant, global communication via the Internet. I mean something *really* extraordinary.

During your lifetime, the people of our culture are going to figure out how to live sustainably on this planet — or they're not. Either way, it's certainly going to be extraordinary. If they figure out how to live sustainably here, then humanity will be able to see something it can't see right now: a future that extends into the indefinite future. If they *don't* figure this out, then I'm afraid the human race is going to take its place among the species that we're driving into extinction here every day — as many as two hundred *every day.*

As people like to say nowadays, you don't have to be a rocket scientist to figure this out. The people who keep track of these things and make it their business to predict such things agree that the human population is going to increase to nine billion by the middle of the century. It isn't just the doomsayers who say this. This is a very conservative estimate, recently endorsed by the UN. Unfortunately, most of the people who make this estimate seem to have the idea that this is workable and okay.

Here's why it isn't.

It's obvious that it costs a lot of money and energy to produce all the food we need to maintain our population at six billion. But there is an additional, hidden cost that has to be counted in *life-forms*. Put plainly, in order to maintain the biomass that is tied up in the six billion of us, we have to gobble up two hundred species a day — in addition to all the food we produce in the ordinary way. We need the biomass of those two hundred species to maintain *this* biomass, the biomass that is in *us*. And when we've gobbled up those species, they're *gone*. Extinct. Vanished forever.

In other words, maintaining a population of six billion humans costs the world two hundred species a day. If this were something that was going to stop next week or next month, that would be okay. But the unfortunate fact is that it's not. It's something that's going to go on happening every day, day after day after day — and that's what makes it unsustainable, *by definition*. That kind of cataclysmic destruction *cannot* be sustained.

The extraordinary thing that is going to happen in the next two or three decades is not that the human race is going to become extinct. The extraordinary thing that's going to happen in the next two or three decades is that a great second renaissance is going to occur. A great and astounding renaissance.

Nothing less than that is going to save us.

THE FIRST RENAISSANCE, the one you met in your history textbooks, was understood to be a rebirth of classical awareness and sensibility. It could hardly have been understood to be what it *actually* was, which was the necessary preface to an entirely new historical era.

A few key medieval ideas were jettisoned during the Renaissance, but they weren't replaced by ideas that would have made sense to classical thinkers. Rather, they were replaced by ideas that were entirely new — ideas that would *not* have made sense to classical thinkers. These were ideas that make would sense to *us*. In fact, these ideas *still* make sense to us.

The Renaissance (and indeed the modern world) came into being because during the fourteenth, fifteenth, and sixteenth centuries an interrelated complex of medieval ideas came under challenge. The centerpiece of the complex related to the means of gaining certain knowledge. During the Middle Ages it was understood that reason and authority were the chief means of gaining certain knowledge. For example, it seemed perfectly reasonable to suppose that the earth was a stationary object around which the rest of the universe revolved. It was reasonable — and it was affirmed by a towering authority, the great second-century astronomer Claudius Ptolemaeus, Ptolemy. Similarly, it seemed perfectly reasonable to suppose that heavy objects fall to earth faster than light objects — and this was affirmed by another towering authority, the polymath genius Aristotle.

But during the Renaissance, reason and authority were toppled as reliable guides to knowledge and replaced by... observation and experimentation. Without this change, science as we know it would not have come into being and the Industrial Revolution would not have occurred.

During the Middle Ages it was taken for granted that our relationship with God was a collective thing that only the Roman Catholic Church was empowered to negotiate. During the Renaissance this dispensation was challenged by a completely new one, in which our relationship with God was seen as an *individual* thing that each of us could negotiate *independently* with God. In this new dispensation was born the magnification and sanctification of the individual that we take for granted in modern times. We all see ourselves as individually valuable and quite fantastically empowered — literally bristling with rights — in a way that would have been astonishing to the people of the Middle Ages.

In the Middle Ages the universe was perceived as a thing that had come into being as a finished object just a few thousand years ago. It was fixed, finite, and as much *known* as it needed to be. In the Renaissance, however, the universe began to be perceived in a much different way: as dynamic, infinite, and largely *unknown*. It was this change in thinking that led not only to the great Age of Exploration but to the great age of scientific investigation that followed and that continues today.

All this seems very obvious to us today. The Middle Ages obviously couldn't last forever. Things obviously *had* to change. But this was not at all obvious to the people of the Middle Ages. As far as they were concerned, people would go on thinking and living the medieval way *forever*.

We think the very same thing. Just like the people of the Middle Ages, we're absolutely sure that people will go on thinking the way we think *forever*, and people will go on living the way we live forever.

The people of the Middle Ages thought this way because it seemed impossible to them that people could think a different way. How else could people think except the way they thought? As far as they were concerned, the history of thought had come to an end *with them*. Of course we smile at that — but in fact we believe exactly the same thing. We, too, believe that the history of thought has come to an end *with us*.

Well, we'd better hope we're wrong about that, because if the history of thought has come to an end with us, then we're doomed. If there are still people here in two hundred years, they won't be living the way we do. I can make that prediction with confidence, because if people go on living the way we do, there won't *be* any people here in two hundred years.

I can make another prediction with confidence. If there are still people here in two hundred years, they won't be *thinking* the way we do. I can make that prediction with equal confidence, because if people go on *thinking* the way we do, then they'll go on *living* the way we do — and there won't *be* any people here in two hundred years.

But what can we possibly change about the way we think? It seems so obvious that everything we think is just the way it *must* be thought.

It seemed exactly the same to the people of the Middle Ages.

Although several key ideas of the Middle Ages disappeared during the Renaissance, not *every* key idea of the Middle Ages disappeared. One of the key ideas that remained in place — and that remains in place today — is the idea that humans are fundamentally and irrevocably flawed. We look at the world around us and find that turtles are not flawed, crows are not flawed, daffodils are not flawed, mosquitoes are not flawed, salmon arc not flawed — in fact, not a single species in the world is flawed — except us. It makes no sense, but it does pass the medieval tests for knowledge. It's reasonable — and it's certainly supported by authority. It's reasonable because it provides us with an excuse we badly need. We're destroying the world — eating it alive — but it's not our fault. It's the fault of human nature. We're just badly made, so what can you expect?

Another key idea that survived the Middle Ages is the idea that the way we live is the way humans are *meant* to live. Well, goodness, that's so obvious it hardly needs saying. We're living the way humans were meant to live from the beginning of time. The fact that we only began living this way very recently has nothing to do with it. So it took us three million years to find it. That doesn't change the fact that it's the way we were meant to live from the beginning of time. And the fact that the way we live is making the world uninhabitable to our own species also has nothing to do with it. Even if we destroy the world and ourselves with it, the way we live is still the way we were meant to live from the beginning of time.

But these two medieval survivors are relatively benign. Stupid but harmless. One other key idea survived, however, that is definitely neither benign nor harmless. Far from being benign or harmless, it's the most dangerous idea in existence. And even more than being the most dangerous *idea* in existence, it's the most dangerous *thing* in existence — more dangerous than all our nuclear armaments, more dangerous than biological warfare, more dangerous than all the pollutants we pump into the air, the water, and the land.

All the same, it *sounds* pretty harmless. You can hear it and say, "Uh-huh, yeah, so?" It's pretty simple, too. Here it is: *Humans belong to an order of being that is separate from the rest of the living community.* There's us and then there's Nature. There's humans and then there's the human environment.

I'm sure it's hard to believe that something as innocent sounding as this could be even a little bit dangerous, much less as dangerous as I've claimed.

As I've said, it's conservatively estimated that as many as two hundred species are becoming extinct *every day* as a result of our impact on the world. People take in this piece of horrendous information very calmly. They don't scream. They don't faint. They don't see any reason to get excited about it because they firmly believe that *humans belong to an order of being that is separate from the rest of the living community.* They believe it as firmly in the twenty-first century as they did in the tenth century.

So as many as two hundred species are becoming extinct every day. That's no problem, because *those* species are *out there* somewhere. Those two hundred species aren't in *here.* They aren't *us.* They don't have anything to *do* with us, because *humans belong to an order of being that is separate from the rest of the living community.*

Those two hundred species are out there in the *environment*. Of course it's bad for the *environment* if they become extinct, but it has nothing to do with *us*. The environment is *out there*, suffering, while we're *in here*, safe and sound. Of course we should try to *take care* of the environment, and it's a shame about those two hundred extinctions — but it has nothing to do with *us*.

Ladies and gentlemen, if people go on thinking this way, humanity is going to become extinct. That's how dangerous this idea is. Here's why.

Those two hundred species . . . why exactly are they becoming extinct? Are they just running out of air or water or space or what? No, those two hundred species are becoming extinct because they have something *we need*. We need their *biomass*. We need the *living stuff* they're made of. We need their biomass in order to maintain *our* biomass. Here's how it works. Go down to Brazil, find yourself a hunk of rain forest, and cut it down or burn it down. Now bring in a herd of cows to pasture there. Or plant potatoes or pineapples or lima beans. All the biomass that was formerly tied up in the birds, insects, and mammals living in that hunk of rain forest is now going into cows, potatoes, pineapples, or lima beans — which is to say into food for *us*.

We *need* to make two hundred species extinct every day in order to maintain the biomass of six billion people. It's not an accident. It's not an oversight. It's not a bit of carelessness on our part. In order to maintain our population of six billion, we need the biomass of two hundred species a day. We are literally turning two hundred species a day into human tissue.

But all too many people — most people, I'm afraid — tend to think, "Well, so what? Humans belong to an order of being that is separate from the rest of the living community. Since we're separate, it doesn't matter how many species we destroy — and since we're superior to them anyway, we're actually improving the world by eliminating them!"

We're like people living in the penthouse of a tall brick building. Every day we need two hundred bricks to maintain our walls, so we go downstairs, knock two hundred bricks out of the walls below, and bring them back upstairs for our own use. Every day . . . every day we go downstairs and knock two hundred bricks out of the walls that are holding up the building we live in. Seventy thousand bricks a year, year after year after year.

I hope it's evident that this is not a sustainable way to maintain a brick building. One day, sooner or later, it's going to collapse, and the penthouse is going to come down along with all the rest.

Making two hundred species extinct every day is similarly not a sustainable way to maintain a living community. Even if we're in some sense at the top of that community, one day, sooner or later, it's going to collapse, and when it does, our being at the top won't help us. We'll come down along with all the rest.

It would be different, of course, if two hundred extinctions a day were just a temporary thing. It's not. And the reason it's not is that, clever as we are, we can't increase the amount of biomass that exists on this planet. We can't increase the amount of land and water that supports life, and we can't increase the amount of sunlight that falls on that land and water. We can *decrease* the amount of biomass that exists on this planet — for example, by making the land sterile or by poisoning the water — but we can't increase it.

All we can do is shift that biomass from one bunch of species to another bunch — and that's what we're doing. We're systematically shifting the biomass of species we *don't* care about into the biomass of species we *do* care about: into cows, chickens, corn, beans, tomatoes, and so on. We're systematically destroying the biodiversity of the living community to support ourselves, which is to say that we're systematically destroying the infrastructure that is keeping us alive.

As I've said, it's conservatively estimated that our population will increase to nine billion by the middle of the century — and people take in this hair-raising piece of information very calmly. No one screams. No one faints. People are as untroubled about our mushrooming population as they are about those two hundred daily extinctions. They see no reason to get excited, because they firmly believe that humans belong to an order of being that is separate from the rest of the living community. They don't see that the extinction rate is going to increase as our population increases — and probably exponentially. This is because when we make species extinct, we don't gain 100 percent of their biomass. A great deal of it is simply lost, contributing to the desertification of the planet. By the middle of the century, if our population has indeed increased to nine billion, then the number of extinctions will be a thousand a day or ten thousand a day (the number is incalculable at this point).

IF THERE ARE still people living here in two hundred years, they'll know that humanity doesn't belong to an order of being that is separate from the rest of the living community. They'll know this as surely as we know that the earth revolves around the sun. I can make this prediction with confidence, because if people go on thinking we belong to a separate order of being, then there *will be* no people living here in two hundred years.

What everyone wishes I could do (and what I myself wish I could do) is describe how people will be living here in two hundred years — if there still *are* people living here. All I can tell you is how they *won't* be living: They won't be living the way we do. But why is that? Why can't I tell you how they *will* be living? The answer is: because no one can tell you that.

You can see why this is so if you put the question back into the Middle Ages. You might very well have been able to convince Roger Bacon that people would be living differently in three hundred years, but how in the world could he have predicted the Age of Exploration, the rebellion against feudal oppression, the Industrial Revolution, the emergence to power of a capitalist bourgeoisie, and so on? To expect such a thing would be absurd.

You could say that if the Middle Ages had been *able* to predict the Renaissance, then it would have *been* the Renaissance.

Social evolution is inherently chaotic — which is another way of saying inherently unpredictable. This is true even in relatively stable times. Consider the fact that every intelligence agency in the world was taken by surprise by the collapse of the Soviet Union, which days before had looked as stable as Great Britain or the United States.

And if social evolution is chaotic in even *stable* times, then it's going to be even more chaotic in the times ahead, when people are either going to start thinking a new way or become extinct.

Of course I understand why people *want* to have a description of the sustainable life of the future. They think this would enable them to adopt that sustainable life *now, today*. But social change doesn't come about that way, any more than technological change does. It would have been useless to show Charles Babbage a printed circuit or to show Thomas Edison a transistor. They could have done nothing with those things in their day — and we could do nothing today with a picture of life a hundred years from now. The future is not something that can be planned hundreds of years in advance — or even ten years in advance. Adolf Hitler's Thousand Year Reich didn't even last a thousand *weeks.* There has never been a plan for the future — and there never will be.

Nevertheless, I can tell you with complete confidence that something extraordinary is going to happen in the next two or three decades. The people of our culture are going to figure out how to live sustainably — or they're not. And either way, it's certainly going to be extraordinary.

The fact that I'm unable to give you a prescription for the future doesn't mean you're just helpless bits of cork bobbing in the tide of history. Each of you is about where Galileo was when he was told in no uncertain terms to shut up about the earth moving around the sun. As far as the gentlemen of the Roman Inquisition were concerned, the earth's movement around the sun was a wicked lie they had to suppress — and *could* suppress. But as he left his trial, Galileo was heard to mutter, "All the same, it moves!"

Surprisingly little hung on the matter. The future of humanity didn't depend on destroying the medieval picture of the solar system. But the future of humanity *does* depend on our destroying the medieval picture of humanity's relationship to the living community of this planet.

Galileo didn't know that people would someday take space travel for granted, but he *did* know that they would someday recognize that the earth revolves around the sun. We don't know how people will live here in two hundred years, but we do know that if people still *are* living here in two hundred years, they will recognize that we are as much a part of the living community — and as thoroughly dependent on it — as lizards or butterflies or sharks or earthworms or badgers or banana trees.

People don't *want* more of the same. Yet, oddly enough, when they ask me what will save the world, they want to *hear* more of the same — something familiar, something recognizable. They want to hear about uprisings or anarchy or tougher laws. But none of those things is going to save us — I wish they could. What we must have — and nothing less — is a whole world *full* of people with changed minds. Scientists with changed minds, industrialists with changed minds, schoolteachers with changed minds, politicians with changed minds — though they'll be the last, of course. Which is why we can't wait for them or expect them to lead us into a new era. Their minds won't change until the minds of their constituents change. Gorbachev didn't create changed minds; changed minds created Gorbachev.

Changing people's minds is something each one of us can do, wherever we are, whoever we are, whatever kind of work we're doing. Changing minds may not seem like a very dramatic or exciting challenge, but it's the challenge that the human future depends on.

It's the challenge *your* future depends on.

Appendix II

Our Religions:
Are They the Religions of Humanity Itself?

Delivered as a Fleming Lecture in Religion,
Southwestern University, Georgetown, Texas, October 18, 2000

CONTRARY TO THE COMMON ASSUMPTION, Charles Darwin did not originate the idea of evolution. By the middle of the nineteenth century the mere *fact* of evolution had been around for a long time, and most thinkers of the time were perfectly content to leave it at that. The absence of a theory to *explain* evolutionary change didn't trouble them, wasn't experienced as a pressure, as it was by Darwin. He knew there had to be some intelligible mechanism or dynamic that would account for it, and this is what he went looking for — with well-known results. In his *Origin of Species* he wasn't announcing the *fact* of evolution; he was trying to make *sense* of the fact.

In my midtwenties I began to feel a similar sort of pressure. The modern Age of Anxiety was just being born under the shadows of rampant population growth, global environmental destruction, and the ever-present possibility of nuclear holocaust. I was surprised that most people seemed perfectly reconciled to these things, as if to say, "Well, what else would you expect?"

Ted Kaczynski, the Unabomber, seemed to think he was saying something terribly original in his 1995 diatribe blaming it all on the Industrial Revolution, but this was just the conventional wisdom of 1962. To my mind, blaming all our problems on the Industrial Revolution is like blaming Hamlet's downfall on his fencing match with Laertes. To understand why Hamlet ended up badly, you can't just look at the last ten minutes of his story, you have to go right back to the beginning of it, and I felt a pressure to do the same with us.

The beginning of *our* story isn't difficult to find. Every schoolchild learns that *our* story began about ten thousand years ago with the Agricultural Revolution. This isn't the beginning of the *human* story, but it's certainly the beginning of *our* story, for it was from this beginning that all the wonders and horrors of our civilization grew.

Everyone is vaguely aware that there have been two ways of looking at the Agricultural Revolution within our culture, two contradictory stories about its significance. According to the standard version — the version taught in our schools — humans had been around for a long time, three or four million years, living a miserable and shiftless sort of life for most of that time, accomplishing nothing and getting nowhere. But then about ten thousand years ago it finally dawned on folks living in the Fertile Crescent that they didn't have to live like beavers and buzzards, making do with whatever food happened to come along; they could cultivate their own food and thus control their own destiny and well-being. Agriculture made it possible for them to give up the nomadic life for the life of farming villagers. Village life encouraged occupational specialization and the advancement of technology on all fronts. Before long villages became towns, and towns became cities, kingdoms, and empires. Trade connections, elaborate social and economic systems, and literacy soon followed, and *there we went.* All these advances were based on — and impossible without — agriculture, manifestly humanity's greatest blessing.

The other story, a much older one, is tucked away in a different corner of our cultural heritage. It, too, is set in the Fertile Crescent and tells a tale of the birth of agriculture, but in this telling agriculture isn't represented as a blessing but rather as a terrible punishment for a crime whose exact nature has always profoundly puzzled us. I'm referring, of course, to the story told in the third chapter of Genesis, the Fall of Adam.

Both these stories are known to virtually everyone who grows up in our culture, including every historian, philosopher, theologian, and anthropologist. But like most thinkers of the mid-nineteenth century, who were content with the mere fact of evolution and felt no pressure to explain it, our historians, philosophers, theologians, and anthropologists seem perfectly content to live with these two contradictory stories. The conflict is manifest but, for them, demands no explanation.

For me, it did. As evolution demanded of Darwin a theory that would make sense of it, the story in Genesis demanded of me a theory that would make sense of it.

There have traditionally been two approaches to Adam's crime and punishment. The text tells us Adam was invited to partake of every tree in the garden of Eden except one, mysteriously called the Tree of the Knowledge of Good and Evil. As we know, Adam succumbed to the temptation to sample this fruit. In one approach, the crime is viewed as simple disobedience, in which case the interdiction of the knowledge of good and evil seems entirely arbitrary. God might just as well have interdicted the knowledge of war and peace or the knowledge of pride and prejudice. The point was simply to forbid Adam *something* in order to test his loyalty. Under this approach, Adam's punishment —

banishment from Eden to live by the sweat of his brow as a farmer — was just a spanking; it doesn't "fit the crime" in any particular way. He would have received this punishment no matter what test he failed.

The second approach tries to make some connection between Adam's crime and his punishment. Under this approach, Eden is viewed as a metaphor for the state of innocence, which is lost when Adam gains the knowledge of good and evil. This makes sense, but only if the knowledge of good and evil is understood as a metaphor for knowledge that *destroys* innocence. So, with roughly equivalent metaphors at either end, the story is reduced to a banal tautology: Adam lost his innocence by gaining knowledge that destroyed his innocence.

The story of the Fall is coupled with a second that is equally famous and equally baffling, that of Cain and Abel. As conventionally understood, these two brothers were literal individuals: the elder, Cain, a tiller of the soil, and the younger, Abel, a herder. The improbability that two members of the same family would embrace antithetical lifestyles should tip us off to the fact that these were not individuals but emblematic figures, just as Adam was (*adam* merely being the Hebrew word for "man").

If we understand these as emblematic figures, then the story begins to make sense. The firstborn of agriculture was indeed the tiller of the soil, as Cain was said to be the firstborn of Adam. This is an undoubted historical fact. The domestication of plants is a process that begins the day you plant your first seed, but the domestication of animals takes generations. So the herder Abel was indeed the second-born — by centuries, if not millennia (another reason to be skeptical of the notion that Cain and Abel were literally second-generation brothers).

A further reason for skepticism on this point is the fact that the ancient farmers and herders of the Near East occupied adjacent but distinctly different regions. Farming was the occupation of the Caucasian inhabitants of the Fertile Crescent. Herding was the occupation of the Semitic inhabitants of the Arabian peninsula to the south.

Another piece of background that needs to be understood is that in very ancient times farmers and herders had radically different lifestyles. Farmers were by the very nature of their work settled villagers; but herders (by the very nature of *their* work) were nomads, just as many present-day herding peoples are. The herding lifestyle was in fact closer to the hunting-gathering lifestyle than it was to the farming lifestyle.

As the farming peoples of the north expanded, it was inevitable that they would confront their Semitic herding neighbors to the south, perhaps below what is now Iraq — with the predictable result. As they have done from the beginning to the present moment, the tillers of the soil needed more land to put to the plow, and as they've done from the beginning to the present moment, they took it.

As the Semites saw it (and it is of course *their* version of the story that we have), the tiller of the soil Cain was watering his fields with the blood of Abel the herder.

The fact that the version we have is the Semitic version explains the central mystery of the story, which is why God rejected Cain's gift but accepted Abel's. Naturally, this is the way the Semites *would* see it. In essence, the story says, "God is on *our* side. God loves us and the way we live but hates the tillers of the soil and the way they live."

With these provisional understandings in place, I was ready to offer a theory about the first part of the story, the Fall of Adam. What the Semitic authors knew was only the *present* fact that their brothers from the north were encroaching on them in a murderous way. They hadn't been physically present in the Fertile

Crescent to witness the actual birth of agriculture, and in fact this was an event that had occurred hundreds of years earlier. In their story of the Fall, they were reconstructing an ancient event, not reporting a recent one. All that was clear to them was that some strange development had saddled their brothers to the north with a laborious lifestyle and had turned them into murderers, and this had to be a moral or spiritual catastrophe of some kind.

What they observed about their brothers to the north was this peculiarity: They seemed to have the strange idea that they knew how to run the world as well as God. This is what marks them as our cultural ancestors. As we go about our business of running the world, we have no doubt that we're doing as good a job as God, if not better. Obviously God put a lot of creatures in the world that are quite superfluous and even pernicious, and we're quite at liberty to get rid of them. We know where the rivers should run, where the swamps should be drained, where the forests should be razed, where the mountains should be leveled, where the plains should be scoured, where the rain should fall. To us, it's perfectly obvious that we have this knowledge.

In fact, to the authors of the stories in Genesis, it looked as if their brothers to the north had the bizarre idea that they had eaten at *God's own tree of wisdom* and had gained the very knowledge God uses to rule the world. And what knowledge is this? It's a knowledge that only God is competent to use, the knowledge that every single action God might take — no matter what it is, no matter how large or small — is *good for one but evil for another.* If a fox is stalking a pheasant, it's in the hands of God whether she will catch the pheasant or the pheasant will escape. If God gives the fox the pheasant, then this is good for the fox but evil for the pheasant. If God allows the pheasant to escape, then this is good for the pheasant but evil for the fox. There's no outcome that can be good for both. The same is true in every area of the world's governance. If God allows the valley to be flooded, then this is good for some but evil for others. If God holds back the flood then this, too, will be good for some but evil for others.

Decisions of this kind are clearly at the very root of what it means to rule the world, and the wisdom to make them cannot possibly belong to any mere creature, for any creature making such decisions would inevitably say, "I will make every choice so that it's good for me but evil for all others." And of course this is precisely how the agriculturalist operates, saying, "If I scour this plain to plant food for myself, then this will be evil for all the creatures that inhabit the plain, but it'll be good for me. If I raze this forest to plant food for myself, then this will be evil for all the creatures that inhabit the forest, but it'll be good for me."

What the authors of the stories in Genesis perceived was that their brothers to the north had taken into their own hands the rule of the world; they had usurped the role of God. Those who let God run the world and take the food that he's planted for them have an easy life. But those who want to run the world themselves must necessarily plant *their own* food, must necessarily make their living by the sweat of the brow. As this makes plain, agriculture was not the crime itself but rather the result of the crime, the punishment that must inevitably follow such a crime. It was wielding the knowledge of good and evil that had turned their brothers in the north into farmers — and into murderers.

But these were not the only consequences to be expected from Adam's act. The fruit of the Tree of the Knowledge of Good and Evil is harmless to God but poison to Man. It seemed to these authors that usurping God's role in the world would be the very death of Man.

And so it seemed to me when I finally worked all this out in the late 1970s. This investigation of the stories in Genesis was not, for me, an exercise in biblical exegesis. I'd gone looking for a way to

188 · If They Give You Lined Paper, Write Sideways

understand how in the world we'd brought ourselves face-to-face with death in such a relatively short period of time — ten thousand years, a mere eyeblink in the life span of our species — and had found it in an ancient story that we long ago adopted as our own and that remained stubbornly mysterious to us as long as we insisted on reading it as if it *were* our own. When examined from a point of view *not* our own, however, it ceased to be mysterious and delivered up a meaning that not only would have made sense to a beleaguered herding people eight thousand years ago but would also make sense to the beleaguered people of the twenty-first century.

As far as I was concerned, the authors of this story had gotten it right. In spite of the terrible mess we've made of it, we *do* think we can run the world, and if we *continue* to think this, it *is* going to be the death of us.

In case it isn't evident, I should add that of course my reading of Genesis is only a theory. This is what creationists say of evolution, that it's "only a theory, it hasn't been proved" — as though this in itself is grounds for dismissal. This misrepresents the point of formulating a theory, which is to make sense of the evidence. So far Darwin's theory remains the very best way we've found to make sense of the evidence, and my own theory has to be evaluated in the same way. Does it make sense of the evidence — the stories themselves — and does it make more sense than any other theory?

BUT SOLVING THIS particular riddle only *began* to alleviate the pressure I felt for answers that were not being looked for at any level of our culture. The philosophical and theological foundations of our culture had been laid down by people who confidently believed that Man had been *born* an agriculturalist and civilization builder. These things were as instinctive to him as predation is to lions or hiving is to bees. This meant that, to find and date Man's birth, they had only to look for the beginnings of agriculture and civilization, which were obviously not that far back in time.

When in 1650 Irish theologian James Ussher announced the date of creation as October 23, 4004 BC, no one laughed, or if they did it was because of the absurd exactitude of the date, not because the date was absurdly recent. In fact, 4004 BC is quite a serviceable date for the beginning of what we would recognize as *civilization*. This being the case, it's hardly surprising that, for people who took it for granted that Man began building civilization as soon as he was created, 4004 BC would seem like a perfectly reasonable date for his creation.

But all this soon changed. By the middle of the nineteenth century the accumulated evidence of many new sciences had pushed almost all dates back by many orders of magnitude. The universe and the earth were not thousands of years old but billions. The human past extended millions of years back beyond the appearance of agriculture and civilization.* The notion that Man had been born an agriculturalist and civilization builder had been rendered totally untenable. He had very definitely not been born either one.

This meant that the philosophical and theological foundations of our culture had been laid by people with a profoundly erroneous understanding of our origins and history. It was therefore urgently important to reexamine these foundations and if necessary to rebuild them from the ground up.

---

*Only those who clung to a very literal reading of the biblical creation story rejected the evidence; they saw it as a hoax perpetrated on us either by the devil (to confound us) or by God (to test our faith) — take your pick.

Except, of course, that no one at all thought this was urgently important — or even slightly important. So human life began millions of years before the birth of agriculture. Who cares? Nothing of any *importance* happened during those millions of years. They were merely a fact, something to be accepted, just as the fact of evolution had been accepted by naturalists long before Darwin.

In the last century we'd gained an understanding of the human story that made nonsense of everything we'd been telling ourselves for three thousand years, but our settled understandings remained completely unshaken. So what, that Man had not in fact been *born* an agriculturalist and a civilization builder? He was certainly born *to become* an agriculturalist and a civilization builder. It was beyond question that this was our foreordained destiny. The way we live is the way humans were *meant* to live from the beginning of time. And indeed we must *go on* living this way — even if it kills us.

Facts that were indisputable to all but biblical literalists had radically repositioned us not only in the physical universe but in the history of our own species. The *fact* that we had been repositioned was all but universally acknowledged, but no one felt any pressure to develop a theory that would make *sense* of the fact, the way Darwin had made sense of the fact of evolution.

Except me, and I have to tell you that it gave me no joy. I had to have answers, and I went looking for them not because I wanted to write a book someday but because I personally couldn't live without them.

In *Ishmael* I made the point that the conflict between the emblematic figures Cain and Abel didn't end six or eight thousand years ago in the Near East. Cain the tiller of the soil has carried his knife with him to every corner of the world, watering his fields with the blood of tribal peoples wherever he found them.

He arrived here in 1492 and over the next three centuries watered his fields with the blood of millions of Native Americans. Today he's down there in Brazil, knife poised over the few remaining aboriginals in the heart of that country.

THE TRIBE AMONG aboriginal peoples is as universal as the flock among geese, and no anthropologist seriously doubts that it was humanity's original social organization. We didn't evolve in troops or hordes or pods. Rather, we evolved in a social organization that was peculiarly human, that was uniquely successful for *culture bearers*. The tribe was successful for humans, which is why it was still universally in place throughout the world three million years later. The tribal organization was natural selection's gift to humanity in the same way that the flock was natural selection's gift to geese.

The elemental glue that holds any tribe together is tribal law. This is easy to say but less easy to understand, because the operation of tribal law is entirely different from the operation of our law. *Prohibition* is the essence of our law, but the essence of tribal law is *remedy*. Misbehavior isn't outlawed in any tribe. Rather, tribal law prescribes what must happen in order to minimize the effect of misbehavior and to produce a situation in which everyone feels that they've been made as whole again as it's possible to be.

In *The Story of B* I described how adultery is handled among the Alawa of Australia. If you have the misfortune to fall in love with another man's wife or another woman's husband, the law doesn't say, "This is prohibited and may not go forward." It says, "If you want your love to go forward, here's what you must do to make things right with all parties and to see to it that marriage isn't cheapened in the eyes of our children." It's a remarkably successful process. What makes it even more remarkable is the fact that it wasn't worked out in any legislature or by any committee. It's another gift of natural selection. Over countless generations of testing, no better way of handling adultery has been found or even conceivably *could* be found, because — *behold!* — it *works!* It does just what the Alawa want it to do, and absolutely no one tries to evade it. Even adulterers don't try to evade it — that's how well it works.

But this is just the law of the Alawa, and it would never occur to them to say, "Everyone in the world should do it this way." They know perfectly well that their tribal neighbors' laws work just as well for them — and for the same reason, that they've been tested from the beginning of time.

One of the virtues of tribal law is that it presupposes that people are just the way we know they are: generally wise, kind, generous, and well intentioned but perfectly capable of being foolish, unruly, moody, cantankerous, selfish, greedy, violent, stupid, bad-tempered, sneaky, lustful, treacherous, careless, vindictive, neglectful, petty, and all sorts of other unpleasant things. Tribal law doesn't punish people for their shortcomings, as our law does. Rather, it makes the management of their shortcomings an easy and ordinary part of life.

But during the developmental period of our culture, all this changed very dramatically. Tribal peoples began to come together in larger and larger associations, and one of the casualties of this process was tribal law. If you take the Alawa of Australia and put them together with Gebusi of New Guinea, the Bushmen of the Kalahari, and the Yanomami of Brazil, they are very literally not going to know how to live. Not any of these tribes are going to embrace the laws of the others, which may be not only unknown to them but incomprehensible to them. How then are they going to handle mischief that occurs among them? The Gebusi way or the Yanomami way? The Alawa way or the

Bushman way? Multiply this by a hundred, and you'll have a fair approximation of where people stood in the early millennia of our own cultural development in the Near East.

When you gather up a hundred tribes and expect them to work and live together, tribal law becomes inapplicable and useless. But of course the people in this amalgam are the same as they always were: capable of being foolish, moody, cantankerous, self-ish, greedy, violent, stupid, bad-tempered, and all the rest. In the tribal situation, this was no problem, because tribal law was *designed* for people like this. But all the tribal ways of handling these ordinary human tendencies had been expunged in our bur-geoning civilization. A new way of handling them had to be invented — and I stress the word *invented*. There was no received, tested way of handling the mischief people were capa-ble of. Our cultural ancestors had to *make something up*, and what they made up were lists of *prohibited* behavior.

Very understandably, they began with the big ones. They weren't going to prohibit moodiness or selfishness. They prohib-ited things like murder, assault, and theft. Of course we don't know what the lists were like until the dawn of literacy, but you can be sure they were in place, because it's hardly plausible that we murdered, robbed, and thieved with impunity for five or six thousand years until Hammurabi finally noticed that these were rather disruptive activities.

When the Israelites escaped from Egypt in the thirteenth cen-tury BC, they were literally a lawless horde, because they'd left the Egyptian list of prohibitions behind. They needed their own list of prohibitions, which God provided — the famous ten. But of course ten didn't do it. Hundreds more followed, but they didn't do it either.

No number has ever done it for us. Not a thousand, ten thou-sand, a hundred thousand. Even millions don't do it, and so every single year we pay our legislators to come up with more. But no matter how many prohibitions we come up with, they never do the trick, because no prohibited behavior has *ever* been eliminated by passing a law against it. Every time someone is sent to prison or executed, this is said to be "sending a message" to miscreants, but for some strange reason the message never arrives, year after year, generation after generation, century after century.

Naturally, we consider this to be a very *advanced* system.

NO TRIBAL PEOPLE has ever been found that claimed *not* to know how to live. On the contrary, they're all completely confident that they know how to live. But with the disappearance of tribal law among us, people began to be acutely aware of *not knowing how to live*. A new class of specialists came to be in demand, their specialty being the enunciation of *how people are supposed to live*. These specialists we call *prophets*.

Naturally it takes special qualifications to be a prophet. You must by definition know something the rest of us *don't* know, something the rest of us are clearly *unable* to know. This means you must have a source of information that is beyond normal reach — or else what good would it be? A transcendent vision will do, as in the case of Siddhartha Gautama. A dream will do, provided it comes from God. But best of all, of course, is direct, personal, unmediated communication with God. The most persuasive and most highly valued prophets, the ones that are worth dying for and killing for, have the word directly from God.

The appearance of religions based on prophetic revelations is unique to our culture. We alone in the history of all humanity needed such religions. We *still* need them (and new ones are being created every day), because we still profoundly feel that we don't know how to live. Our religions are the peculiar creation of a bereft people. Yet we don't doubt for a moment that they are the religions of humanity itself.

This belief was not an unreasonable one when it first took root among us. Having long since forgotten that humanity was here long before we came along, we assumed that we were humanity itself and that our history was human history itself. We imagined that humanity had been in existence for just a few thousand years — and that God had been talking to us from the beginning. So why *wouldn't* our religions be the religions of humanity itself?

When it became known that humanity was millions of years older than we, no one thought it odd that God had remained aloof from the thousands of generations that had come before us. Why would God bother to talk to *Homo habilis* or *Homo erectus*? Why would he bother to talk even to *Homo sapiens* — until *we* came along? God wanted to talk to *civilized* folks, not savages, so it's no wonder he remained disdainfully silent.

The philosophers and theologians of the nineteenth and twentieth centuries weren't troubled by God's long silence. The fact alone was enough for them, and they felt no pressure to develop a theory to make sense of it. For Christians, it had long been accepted that Christianity was humanity's religion (which is why all of humanity had to be converted to it, of course). It was an effortless step for thinkers like Teilhard de Chardin and Matthew Fox to promote Christ from humanity's Christ to the Cosmic Christ.

Very strangely, it remained to me to recognize that there once *was* a religion that could plausibly be called the religion of humanity. It was humanity's first religion and its only *universal* religion, found wherever humans were found, in place for tens of thousands of years. Christian missionaries encountered it wherever they went, and piously set about destroying it. By now it has been all but stamped out either by missionary efforts or more simply by exterminating its adherents. I certainly take no pride in its discovery, since it's been in plain sight to us for hundreds of years.

Of course it isn't accounted a "real" religion, since it isn't one of ours. It's just a sort of half-baked "pre-religion." How could it be anything else, since it emerged long before God decided humans were worth talking to? It wasn't revealed by any accredited prophet, has no dogma, no evident theology or doctrine, no liturgy, and produces no interesting heresies or schisms. Worst of all, as far as I know no one has ever killed for it or died for it — and what sort of religion is *that?* Considering all this, it's actually quite remarkable that we even have a name for it.

The religion I'm talking about is, of course, animism. This name was cut to fit the general missionary impression that these childlike savages believe that things like rocks, trees, and rivers have spirits in them, and it hasn't lost this coloration since the middle of the nineteenth century.

Needless to say, I wasn't prepared to settle for this trivialization of a religion that flourished for tens of thousands of years among people exactly as smart as we are. After decades of trying to understand what these people were telling us about their lives and their vision of humanity's place in the world, I concluded that a very simple (but far from trivial) worldview was at the foundation of what they were saying: *The world is a sacred place, and humanity belongs in such a world.*

It's simple but also deceptively simple. This can best be seen if we contrast it with the worldview at the foundation of our own religions. In the worldview of our religions, the world is anything but a sacred place. For Christians, it's merely a place of testing and has no intrinsic value. For Buddhists it's a place where suffering is inevitable. If I oversimplify, my object is not to misrepresent but only to clarify the general difference between these two worldviews in the few minutes that are left to me.

For Christians, the world is not where humans *belong*; it's not our true home, it's just a sort of waiting room where we pass the time before moving on to our *true* home, which is heaven. For Buddhists, the world is another kind of waiting room, which we visit again and again in a repeating cycle of death and rebirth until we finally attain liberation in nirvana.

For Christians, if the world *were* a sacred place, we wouldn't belong in it, because we're all sinners; God didn't send his only-begotten son to make us worthy of living in a sacred world but to make us worthy of living with God in heaven. For Buddhists, if the world were a sacred place, then why would we strive to escape it? If the world were a sacred place, then would we not rather *welcome* the repeating cycle of death and rebirth?

From the animist point of view, humans belong in a sacred place because they themselves are sacred. Not sacred in a special way, not *more* sacred than anything else, but merely *as* sacred as anything else — as sacred as bison or salmon or crows or crickets or bears or sunflowers.

This is by no means all there is to say about animism. It's explored more fully in *The Story of B*, but this, too, is just a beginning. I'm not an authority on animism. I doubt there could ever *be* such a thing as an authority on animism.

SIMPLE IDEAS ARE NOT always easy to understand. The very simplest idea I've articulated in my work is probably the least understood: *There is no one right way for people to live — never has been and never will be.* This idea was at the foundation of tribal life everywhere. The Navajo never imagined that they had the *right* way to live (and that all others were *wrong*). All they had was a way that suited *them*. With tribal peoples on all sides of them — all living in different ways — it would have been ridiculous for them to imagine that theirs was the one right way for people to live. It would be like us imagining that there is one right way to orchestrate a Cole Porter song or one right way to make a bicycle.

In the tribal world, because there was complete agreement that no one had the *right* way to live, there was a staggering glory of cultural diversity, which the people of our culture have been tirelessly eradicating for ten thousand years. For us, it will be paradise when everyone on earth lives *exactly the same way*.

Almost no one blinks at the statement that there is no one right way for people to live. In one of his denunciations of scribes and pharisees, Jesus said, "You gag on the gnat but swallow down the camel." People find many gnats in my books to gag on, but this great hairy camel goes down as easily as a teaspoon of honey.

May the forests be with you and with your children.